C000092692

Tarot

An Essential Beginner's Guide to Psychic Tarot Reading, Tarot Card Meanings, Tarot Spreads, Numerology, and Astrology

© **Copyright 2019**

All Rights Reserved. No part of this book may be reproduced in any form without permission in writing from the author. Reviewers may quote brief passages in reviews.

Disclaimer: No part of this publication may be reproduced or transmitted in any form or by any means, mechanical or electronic, including photocopying or recording, or by any information storage and retrieval system, or transmitted by email without permission in writing from the publisher.

While all attempts have been made to verify the information provided in this publication, neither the author nor the publisher assumes any responsibility for errors, omissions or contrary interpretations of the subject matter herein.

This book is for entertainment purposes only. The views expressed are those of the author alone, and should not be taken as expert instruction or commands. The reader is responsible for his or her own actions.

Adherence to all applicable laws and regulations, including international, federal, state and local laws governing professional licensing, business practices, advertising and all other aspects of doing business in the US, Canada, UK or any other jurisdiction is the sole responsibility of the purchaser or reader.

Neither the author nor the publisher assumes any responsibility or liability whatsoever on the behalf of the purchaser or reader of these materials. Any perceived slight of any individual or organization is purely unintentional.

Contents

Introduction

Have you always been interested in tarot, but you just didn't know where to start? Have you wondered if you were psychic and had no way to test it out? Have you had a tarot deck sitting on your shelf for ages that you haven't touched because you weren't sure? If you've answered "yes" to any of these questions, this book is the one for you!

Welcome to *Tarot: An Essential Beginner's Guide to Psychic Tarot Reading, Tarot Card Meanings, Tarot Spreads, Numerology, and Astrology*. Welcome, and congratulations for downloading this book. You will not regret doing so, for the following pages are full of information you can use to not only understand the tarot (finally!) but to literally change your life.

The book will begin with an examination of the history of tarot cards and their usage across time in Chapter 1 before going into the art of the tarot itself in Chapter 2. In that second chapter, you'll learn about how to connect with your intuition, how to choose a deck, and what the pros and cons of tarot happen to be.

Chapter 3 introduces you to all 78 cards in the tarot deck before providing some tips and tricks for memorization. Chapter 4 reveals 20 different spreads you can use for your own tarot readings, and Chapter 5 provides 10 exercises and brain boosters for your practice (as well as 3 overall tips for the tarot trade).

Chapter 6 demonstrates how tarot is intimately connected with numerology and astrology; then Chapter 7 discloses a method you can use to make tarot a part of your career in the future. By the end of this book, you should feel that you've received all the information you need to be able to read tarot cards for yourself and others. You should feel confidently psychic and ready to take on the world!

Chapter 1: Tarot History

Tarot is essentially a card game designed to tell fortunes and reveal the future. It didn't start off that way, though! At first, tarot was simply a deck of cards for playing card games socially. At first, tarot decks were only comprised of those original 56 cards, and they hardly looked anything like they do today.

In the early days of tarot, the deck was rather simple. With no Major Arcana section whatsoever, there were just the court/face cards and the remaining 40 suited cards, with each suit counting ace-10. The early days of tarot were also likely not as ancient as you'd like to think. Early days of tarot were simply the late 14th and early 15th centuries.

Tarot Practices Across Time

While many ancient cultures surely had their own means of divination, it is unlikely that the actual tarot deck of today existed anywhere across time except from around the turn of the 15th century. There is no archaeological proof of this long-time connection, and we have virtually no historical proof of the tarot's existence unless we look at Europe around the 15th century.

Despite this concrete history – which places the first tarot decks being released and played (casually, as a card game; not as a divination tool) around 1375 – it is possible that the ancient mysteries and archetypes revealed by the Major Arcana cards especially – which weren't added to the deck until around 1450 – may have actually been passed down from ancient cultures across the world.

The symbols in the tarot seem older than time itself. Perhaps this is why people freely speculate about tarot being older than history can prove. Perhaps this is why people across the world can relate to the cards. The symbols speak to us in ways we often can't put words to, and that's the essence of divination. Interestingly enough, however, these images on both the Major *and* Minor Arcana cards were added to the deck much later.

I already explained how the Major Arcana section of the deck came later, around 1450, as opposed to when the tarot was "invented," around 1350. However, it is useful to explain this history a little more. Tarot was originally played as a parlor game called Triumph that was similar to Bridge today, and that game had absolutely no divination intent. However, with growing interest in divination in Europe around the turn of the 17th century, people began to associate their own, much deeper meanings to the cards.

At this time, the deck would have consisted of a detailed Major Arcana section with a far simpler Minor Arcana section, and the court/face cards may have been beautiful, but the pip cards (numbering ace-10) would have been extremely simple with just the cups, swords, wands, and coins – nothing else. Even around the turn of the 19th century, the deck was still incredibly simple, without much adornment on those pip cards, but people were *much* more fascinated in the tarot as a means of divination than anything else at this time.

In fact, the first divination-only tarot deck was designed and released on the European market by Jean-Baptiste Alliette in 1791. This French occultist developed the imagery on the Major Arcana and court/face cards extensively, but the pip cards were still largely neglected. It wasn't until the turn of the 20th century that a follower of Aleister Crowley's philosophy, Arthur Waite, teamed up with fellow occultist and artist Pamela Colman Smith in order to design the cards as we know them today. At this point, tarot got its first distinctly American influences, and the study of tarot increased in popularity, allowing it to spread across the world like wildfire.

Waite insisted on the importance of including people and imagery on the pip cards as well as all the others, if not for any other reason than to give the card readers at home a little more to work with on those previously basic cards. Smith's artwork was finalized, and the deck was released to the world under the name of the Rider-Waite deck, although some still call it the Waite-Smith deck in recognition of the artist herself.

Debate Over Origins

There are legends about the first tarot deck originating in Ancient Egypt. Popular theories from the late 18th century tend to support this claim, but there's not much actual history behind this connection. It was in 1781 that a Frenchman named Antoine Court de Gebelin claimed this ancient Egyptian connection through a paper he had published. He was convinced that the images on the Major Arcana cards were taken directly from the mythology and cosmology of Ancient Egypt. He even claimed that the Catholic Church and the popes knew of this age-old connection and that they wanted desperately to keep it hidden. Of course, people at the time loved this story, and despite its lack of historical background, they bought it hook, line, and sinker.

There are legends that the tarot deck originated in Gypsy culture. People see the mystical images on the cards and associate them with the eccentricity and occultism they stereotypically expect from gypsies across time. Popular culture hasn't helped with these stereotypes either. There are frequent depictions in films of gypsies with tarot decks or of them simply reading peoples' fortunes. And while gypsies surely had their own nomadic/indigenous styles of earth magic and divination, if they *were* associated with tarot decks, it was probably because someone picked up a deck of parlor playing cards and then infused it with his or her own meaning. Tarot wouldn't have been all that accessible to gypsies otherwise unless someone was able to make his or her own deck from scratch.

There are legends that the tarot deck originated from Kabbalistic Jewish practice. The Major Arcana's symbols match the same number as paths to follow in the Kabbalah's Tree of Life. There are 22 of each, and the symbols align almost perfectly. People love to speculate that the imagery and symbolism were meant to be aligned because these cards were first designed by these people, but that historical hunch is incredibly hard to prove. It's much more likely that the rise of occultist interest around the turn of the 20th century in Europe influenced tarot deck artists (and therefore, the way the cards looked) to create decks that *appeared* as if more Kabbalistic secrets had been infused all along. Surely, around this time, Hermetic Mysticism crept into the deck as well, and Egyptian symbolism, mythology, and cosmology have already been infused into the deck almost a century before.

There are even legends that the tarot deck originated around the (decidedly less ancient) time of the Cathars, circa 1150. The Cathars were a practicing sect of Christianity that believed Roman Catholicism worshipped idols and held impure beliefs about their own power. They practiced a much more orthodox sect of Christianity, but it was also somehow more aligned with what we today see as the "occult." These Cathars believed in reincarnation, practicing rituals, and the ancient mysteries of this Earth. Some people, therefore, think that Cathars may have produced the first images for the Major Arcana cards (although, in reality, those cards weren't produced until around three centuries later).

Tarot decks are not as pure and ancient as we once thought. It turns out they've been altered and adapted greatly over time, too, which is perhaps a part of why their exact origin feels so difficult to pinpoint. Additionally, the tarot's images are poignant, and their symbolistic meanings feel ubiquitous, reaching across language and cultural barriers to express truths about humanity as a whole. Tarot certainly feels ancient. I would have believed that tarot arose out of Ancient Egypt if someone I trusted insisted on it, but that's why doing your own research can be so important and validating.

The history of tarot proves that tracking down the deck's exact origins is complicated, an enfolding process like trying to escape from a maze. The more you think you know, the more there is to correct your thinking. Regardless of where and when the tarot arose, however, it's here for us today, and its abilities to help us are extensive. There are so many possibilities to do with the spread or layouts of cards. You can get so many different kinds of decks these days. You can take classes to learn more about tarot, both online and in person. You can download apps on your devices devoted to tarot so you can learn on the go. It almost doesn't matter where tarot came from because it's clearly a constant work in progress that keeps getting strengthened, enhanced, and adapted through time. As you can, just be grateful that it's here for you today, relax and feel supported by this knowledge, grab a nearby deck of tarot cards, and let them connect you with your fate.

Chapter 2: The Art of Tarot

Regardless of how old it is exactly, tarot is a divinatory art that uses symbols, numbers, and connections to the collective unconscious in order to express its meaning. It's designed like a card game with 78 cards, versus the standard deck with 52 cards. It's not played like a standard deck of cards, either. Tarot relies on ancient mysteries to establish its visual truth, and by arranging the cards in a certain fashion, you can receive insight into your issues or illnesses, and you can obtain messages from your higher self and the universe.

Connecting to Intuition

Tarot card reading is so much more about connecting to one's higher self than it is about divining the inherent truth of the cards. The cards always contain the same images and the same basic meanings, but by *your* shuffling and intentional questioning of the deck, the cards group into arrangements that reveal deep and lasting truths that will resonate only for the querent. However, it must be emphasized that the cards are not the entities that hold power with tarot, and neither is the querent (the person you're drawing cards *for* or *about*). The *reader* of the cards is that entity, and his or her higher self is the center of that power.

When you decide that you're ready to embrace tarot and start reading the cards, remember this truth as you proceed. It doesn't necessarily matter what deck you choose, for it's much more important *how* you use the cards of any deck. Use the deck for healing and growth purposes, and it will never do anyone harm. There are certainly rumors that tarot is evil, unholy, or that it invites in spirits that can hurt you. I say now, firmly, tarot isn't about that. Tarot is simply about the reader of the cards connecting with his or her higher self in an effort to answer questions and to heal.

When you engage in your own readings of the cards, remember the importance of your intuition, for it is your direct channel to your higher self. If you ever feel that something I've written doesn't jive with your intuition, please don't force yourself to accept it! Your intuition is your highest truth, and it is much more valuable to you than my words are. If indeed you *do* have this experience with any guidance or associations I elucidate, make a note in your own tarot journal or the pages of this book (if you've chosen to print it). Keep record of these insights, for they are so endlessly helpful for you, both now and in the future.

Choosing Your Deck

Choosing your deck is one of the most fun (although sometimes stressful) moments for the beginning practitioner of tarot. There is certainly a number to choose from. If you're looking at decks online, there are probably *hundreds* of options. If you're looking at your local bookstore or metaphysical store, there are still a lot, but hopefully not quite so many. As you go about making these choices, follow the guidelines below for some assistance.

How to Apply Intuition

Remember that your intuition is your inherent connection with your higher self. As you strive to choose a tarot deck for yourself, it's so essential that you learn to let your intuition be your guide. Whether you're shopping online or in person, try this exercise to apply your intuition to the task:

> Gather 3-4 potential tarot decks that you really like. Hold the options in-hand (or in your real or virtual shopping cart). Sit with these options for a while and try to turn off your thinking mind. Almost enter a meditative state as you take in your options and reject any logic-based choices. You want the choice to arise totally naturally as if it's been your truth all along.

Psychic Choices

If you're having trouble using your intuition, you can go a step further to see what your psychic choice would be. It might seem counter-intuitive that making a psychic choice would be easier than making an intuitive choice, but the trick in this instance is your eyes. When you're working through intuition, you'll want to keep your eyes open so that you're using some part of your mind to make the selection. It's important that you struggle through what's logical versus what's deeper, truer, and emotional.

When you're working through psychic potential, however, you'll want those eyes 100% shut. Close off your physical body to any influences whatsoever, and let your psychic powers guide your choice. Again, this method works for both in-store and online shopping. For online shoppers, gather all the potential items in your "shopping cart," close your eyes, spin around a few times if you can, and then point out the deck that's meant to be yours. Open your eyes at the very end to see which one you selected.

Types of Decks

There are so many different kinds of decks that it's almost overwhelming to approach. For your ease, it will help to know that some decks are specifically tarot decks while some will say they are "Oracle Decks." These Oracle decks are totally different. While the tarot has 78 cards, divided between 22 Major Arcana and 56 Minor Arcana, Oracle decks can have any number of cards, and each one is like its own Major Arcana card with impressive themes and meanings. Additionally, there are no court/face cards, and no numbered "pip" cards (like the 4 of Wands, 8 of Cups, etc.) in an Oracle deck. Overall, I'd steer clear of Oracle decks if you truly want to work with tarot (although Oracle decks are equally awesome and fun in their own right).

Another tip is that some tarot decks are oriented toward themes that may not resonate with you. There are black cat tarot decks, Egyptian-themed tarot decks, gay culture tarot decks, "Animal Wisdom" tarot decks, David Bowie-themed tarot decks, unicorn tarot decks, medieval-themed tarot decks, renaissance-themed tarot decks, wartime tarot decks, "Wild Unknown" tarot decks, "Tarot Apokalypsis" decks, Age of Aquarius tarot decks, Druid-themed tarot decks, animals & nature tarot decks, Illuminati tarot decks, and so much more. Finally, there are the basic decks that use the same essential imagery from the Rider-Waite tarot deck with just a unique flourish from the artist. (The Rider-Waite tarot deck was designed and released in 1909 and is the most basic, most traditional deck still produced in mass today).

Furthermore, there are decks with large-sized cards versus small-sized cards, and I always recommend that bigger cards are better (especially for starting practitioners!). There are also decks that come with their own explanatory books, while there are decks that come alone. I prefer the ones with the attached books – I can never get enough tarot books, though!

much later

Pros & Cons

Generally, follow these pros & cons as you decide which deck will be yours.

Pros:

- Large card size
- Relatable theme
- No discernable theme
- Package comes with a detailed book
- Definitely a tarot deck (not an Oracle deck)
- Relatable art
  - A note on this point: Some tarot decks only show white people, and that won't matter for some, but it will absolutely ostracize other practitioners. The reader of the cards must be able to relate to the art on the cards, so seek out art that reflects your skin color if you can. Again, this note is more helpful for some than others, for I know that some people won't be bothered by this element whatsoever.
- The deck seemingly chose you
- Good paper quality
- Attached book is large, extensive, detailed, and well-written
- Good reviews of the product (for online shoppers)
- Good card thickness
- Perfectly affordable within your means

Cons:

- Cards are too small
- Not a relatable theme for you
- Theme is too "loud" in the cards / is distracting
- No book comes with the package

- It's an Oracle deck, not a tarot deck
- Not relatable art
- Someone chose the deck for you / you don't think it chose you
- Poor paper quality
- Attached book is small or poorly-written
- Poor reviews of the product (for online shoppers)
- Cards feel too thick or too thin
- Not affordable within your current means

Reading the Cards

Now that you've received some assistance in choosing your deck, you're going to need to understand exactly what you're getting yourself into. Tarot is a beautiful divination art that allows you to connect with realms deep within and far outside the self. It's a helpful tool used to provide growth, balance, support, and flourishing to anyone's life. There are so many different things you can do with a tarot deck, too. It might all look the same for you're always just shuffling cards and drawing some out of the deck, but the *intention* behind these acts can vary significantly to the potential benefit of so many people.

Decision Making

Tarot is an excellent tool to boost one's decision-making abilities. So many people these days are indecisive or unsure how to resolve large issues that loom over their lives. So many people, too, are hoping for growth but don't know the right direction. Tarot can provide that decision, resolution, growth, direction, and more, with hardly anything done on the individual's part aside from placing one's hands on the deck and asking a question to the universe. Tarot can help you make the tough choices that you face, and truly enables anyone to regain control over   his or her life from here on out. From now on, with the assistance of tarot, you'll be able to:

- Choose your life path with confidence;
- Learn how to own up to your mistakes;
- Uncover the reasons behind your anxieties, fears, and diseases;
- Make simple decisions easier through 1- to 5-card pulls;
- Discern your motivation;
- Assess most likely outcomes;
- Assert your values and ideal situations;
- and so much more.

Quality of Life

Tarot can remind you that you are in control of your life. It often feels like we're being thrown through situations and experiences like a rag doll, but we as humans have an incredible amount of free will! When you ask questions of the tarot, the answers provided come from the reader's higher self, and they are almost always inflected with divine intention. Therefore, these answers are not going to direct you toward failure or floundering or loss. They're only going to urge you toward growth, but it's up to *you* to choose whether or not you follow the path revealed to you by the cards. Look forward to the following benefits to your life after working with tarot:

- Enhanced compassion and empathy for others;
- Amplified ability to empower yourself and others;
- Developed, honed, and focused psychic abilities;
- Increased potential for creativity and creative expression;
- Enhanced self-awareness and consciousness of the world;
- Increased trust in your intuition and higher self;
- Better understanding of how much will power one has;
- and so much more.

Insight & Life Help

Tarot can also generally provide insight into one's circumstances and assist anyone in need (whether they're in need of direction, assistance, clarity, or otherwise). Tarot spreads are perfectly designed for this task, and you will find 20 detailed spreads to choose from in Chapter 4. Furthermore, by connecting the reader with his or her intuition, psychic abilities, and higher self, that person will be aided deeply. Additionally, both readers and querents will experience increased and enhanced abilities to heal and receive guidance from the universe. Ask the cards one short question or a long, detailed one. You're sure to receive helpful insights and tidbits for refreshed direction in the future.

Helping Others & World Healing

As you master the tarot, you'll be increasingly knowledgeable, empathetic, and willing to help others. You'll find your capacity for patience boosted, and as a reader of the cards, you'll carry great responsibility to share this patience and fresh knowledge with others. With this knowledge, you'll also carry information about the greatest archetypal energies known to humankind across time. You will carry the stories, you will bear the burdens, but you will also hold the key that unchains all our shackles. As you grow in your knowledge and appreciation of tarot, don't be afraid to ask questions that will benefit individuals, whole groups of people, or the Earth as a planet and nurturing entity. Widen your scope, open your eyes, and proceed bravely without fear. With knowledge comes great responsibility, but don't worry – I guarantee you'll love every minute of it.

Chapter 3: The Cards

The most essential part of understanding the tarot is being able to access the meanings of the cards themselves. What does the Emperor mean? What is the suit of Cups all about? What's a Page of Swords? What's an Ace mean in this deck? What if I pull a card that's upside-down? All these questions and more will be answered in this chapter, and you will end this section feeling confident that there's a substantial well of knowledge to draw from when you conduct your first tarot readings.

Major Arcana

The Major Arcana, also called the Greater Arcana, reveals the inner mysteries of humanity. They tell the story of humanity in the form of 22 archetypal images, and each piece of the story reveals deep truths about the nature of existence as a human in this reality. The 22 cards in the Major Arcana are numbered from 0-21 or 1-22. Occasionally, the Major Arcana starts with 0 (the Fool), but I've listed the Fool last here, as number 22, which is equally common. The point with the Fool is that it begins the cycle and when that cycle ends, the Fool starts it up again; therefore, it exists on both extremes and earns its right to be both 0 and 22.

Some decks will have a "Major Arcana" section with numbered cards 1-22 without these same card names. Worry not – the archetypes are still always the same in deeper meaning. Even with different names, card 1 from the Major Arcana will always represent what the Magician does; card 2 will always relate to the High Priestess's energy, card 3 will always signify the Empress's energy, and so on.

For your convenience, in this chapter, I've explained what each card means when it's right-side-up as well as when it's upside-down. When you pull a card upside-down, it's called "in reverse," and it typically lessens the effect of the card in question, but occasionally, it means that matters will be more intense than what the card describes.

1. The Magician

The Magician is all about seeing your path ahead, making decisions, and

taking actions. This card signifies that it's time to follow your dreams. There has been time for introspection, but now is the time for action. The Magician represents a powerful source of inspiration that is ready to act as your muse, and it predicts that you will be able to work on complex projects at this time. This card stands for finding your flow, taking first steps, becoming empowered, embracing your will power, activating your energy, following direction, and engaging in creativity. Power and success lie ahead.

In reverse, the Magician signifies that your flow has become blocked. There are projects you dream of that just aren't working out. It might not be your fault, so look at the cards that appear around the Magician in reverse to find clues to this issue.

2. The High Priestess

The High Priestess card is all about appreciating the feminine in the world.

This card suggests the value of stillness, contemplation, passivity, sensitivity, reflection, and depth. This card tells you that you can manifest your dreams as long as you're open to the mysterious feminine energy within you. Overall, the High Priestess stands for the divine feminine, initiation, gateways, the collective unconscious, true wisdom, dream guidance, and powerful intuition.

In reverse, the High Priestess signifies that you'll need to take a step back

in life in order to access this divine feminine grace and insight. You might need to tone things down, or you may be caught up in delusions that distract you from this capacity. It's time to find stillness and refocus so that things don't turn disastrous.

3. The Empress

The Empress card suggests that abundance is headed your way. This card

represents the potential of abundance through reproduction as well as financial prosperity in your life and more. For those invested in the reproductive meaning, this card signifies fertility, creation, and the product of two true lovers. For those divested from this meaning, this card is still incredibly significant. It represents fertile ideas that exist within you and the potential for you to use them (likely soon!) in order to change your circumstances for the better.

In reverse, the Empress signifies a blockage to your creative expression.

Upside-down, this card represents impotence, infertility, poverty, repressed truth, and lack of what is, in essence, the Empress herself. With these blockages in place, you will struggle to achieve the abundance the Empress wants to offer you. Look to the surrounding cards for clues regarding how to remove these blockages!

4. The Emperor

The Emperor card represents the quintessential divine masculine. It is

about power, fatherhood, leadership, protection, order, and successful accomplishments. Pulling this card in a reading suggests that success is imminent. As long as you use the strength of your will and your clear, focused intellect, you can achieve anything you set your mind to. This card can also represent a father figure or paternal entity in your life that you may or may not be getting along well with.

In reverse, the Emperor signifies what happens when authority is lost.

Perhaps tyranny occurs — perhaps unproductive revolution. Perhaps lack of center and perhaps additional strength. The outcome is up to you. Furthermore, this reversal can represent the loss of a father figure, lack of focus, indecision, or lack of self-worth in relation to your dreams. It could also be a clue that you've been overly judgmental against others recently.

5. The Hierophant

The Hierophant card represents the importance of learning, tradition, and

routine. This card will appear in a reading to remind you to take counsel of those you trust most before making major decisions. Furthermore, it will remind you to value those people whose counsel you utterly trust. The Hierophant encourages the following of established traditions, but he also accepts that there is a limitation in tradition that some cannot withstand. For those individuals, this card represents what may stand in your way to success. For those who accept and embrace tradition, this card represents the beginning of your journey to self-actualization.

In reverse, the Hierophant signifies what happens when tradition goes out

the window: chaos, rebellion, and free-flow of wisdom. While this situation may sound entirely beneficial to some, structure in the sharing of wisdom is much preferred to free-flow, and systems are more effective when they're in place than they are when they're in ruins. Watch out for rejection or a shifting in values.

6. The Lovers

The card of the Lovers represents that love is headed your way. However,

it insists that you cannot handle love if you're not able to first love and appreciate yourself. The Lovers can be a signal that your twin flame is headed into your life, but it could also represent the urgent need for you to fall in love with yourself as your own twin flame. This card insists we appreciate the logic that the heart holds dear, for it is more valuable than many could ever imagine.

In reverse, the Lovers signify that struggles in love are ahead. Whether it's

indecision, jealousy, unrequited or chaotic love, separation, or impotence, something's about to be disturbed in your romantic haven. If you don't have a partner, it could be that some issues are arising in your personality that are keeping you from experiencing self-love. Look to surrounding cards for clues as to how you can fix the situation.

7. The Chariot

The Chariot card signifies that any issues you're working through will be

resolved in a short time. It suggests that embracing control of your life will allow you to find both the peace and the change you desire in the situation. The Chariot insists on growth, mastery, success, triumph, journeying, development, and understanding. However, none of this success can happen without first struggling through conflict, so the Chariot card also assumes that trials have happened recently (or are happening) that will soon be resolved. The Chariot shows how even a successful person is a work in progress.

In reverse, the Chariot signifies interruptions in your path to success or

blatant failures that stand in your way. It can also symbolize a loss of, or general lack of, control that leads to burnout. This card can represent upcoming danger, but it's often a danger that will only affect your personality. Without careful consideration and alteration to your circumstances, you will stagnate, and your growth will be disastrously interrupted.

8. Strength

The Strength card – with its image of a brave woman standing beside a

large beast – demonstrates the peace of the Goddess that exists within every person. Both men and women have goddess blessings within that express as patience, understanding, compassion, and charisma. This card signals that those blessings are present and working to your advantage. Furthermore, Strength signifies the importance of faith and courage, even for feminine individuals. Strength reminds us all to get back in touch with our inner wildness in order to honor our highest selves.

In reverse, Strength signifies a lack of courage that borders on fear.

Instead of being brave and accessing one's blessings, this card in reverse symbolizes that one is experiencing torment, hopelessness, and failed integrations (of any lessons the universe has presented). If you pull Strength in reverse, look out for places in your life where weakness or indecision could be holding you back, find stillness, and carefully examine your emotions and thoughts for clues about how to move forward.

9. The Hermit

The Hermit card is a powerful indicator that intense transformation lies

ahead, but it also suggests that you will need to spend serious time alone to embrace that transformative path. The Hermit forces you to face those spiritual and emotional elements in your life that are likely holding you back. Furthermore, this card reminds you of your connection to your higher self. Once you access that alone time, this connection will be both strengthened and developed so that it's more useful to you than ever. If you pull the Hermit card, it's time to withdraw, get introspective, and retreat into your own psyche for a little while. When you re-emerge, you will be like a butterfly emerging from its caterpillar cocoon.

In reverse, the Hermit signifies the worst that can happen with alone time:

isolation, ostracism, fear, loneliness, and stagnation. If you pull the Hermit in reverse, look closely at your social patterns to see if you've been too isolated to sustain growth. Sometimes, this alone time starts out healthy and turns toxic, as with moments after betrayal, crisis, or breakup. To ensure things remain productive, embrace this shadow time as a temporary thing that will inevitably lead to growth, rather than seeing it as a moment to inhabit for eternity.

10. The Wheel of Fortune

The Wheel of Fortune card suggests that bounty is coming! It shows how

you can reap the rewards of your current situation by channeling prosperity and by embracing inevitability. To receive this card in a reading means that one season of the self is ending to make way for the next, more powerful season. The Wheel of Fortune represents the Hermit's wisdom, and introspection put into action. It's the next step after the Hermit's necessary isolation, which is the actualization of the individual's soul mission.

In reverse, the Wheel of Fortune signifies that you're being faced with

change but fiercely ignoring it. This card shows how your internal harvest may have been bittersweet (or perhaps more bitter than sweet whatsoever) rather than productive. Additionally, there may be more difficult times ahead before you're able to grow. The trick to the situation may be allowing yourself the freedom to let go of what no longer serves.

11. Justice

The Justice card represents that there's a clear path to success in your

vicinity. You'll have to access balance and clarity, however, in order to find that path. Furthermore, you'll have to learn, intimately, your own truth. Those who pull Justice should know that an important dilemma will surface in your life shortly, and your choice will determine so much. Make sure that you're actively *choosing* in response to the dilemma rather than just *reacting* to the options instinctually. Take the time to think things out and embrace what is truly best.

In reverse, Justice signifies the existence of imbalance, dishonesty, and

unfairness in reference to both the self and others. If you pull this card, look to your life to find what's causing imbalance. Open a wide, discerning, introspective eye toward yourself to see where injustice or unfairness may be controlling your actions unintentionally.

12. The Hanged Man

The Hanged Man card represents your experience becoming intensified,

refocused, deepened, or expanded. The Hanged Man on the card hangs upside-down, and this positioning represents a paradigm shift and a complete perspective upheaval. However, this shifting and upheaval is nothing but positive. If you draw this card, your future holds a huge reversal that will draw good things and progress your way. Expect upheavals, shifting, and transformations, but don't be afraid! By drawing this card, it signifies that you may even be set to experience a shaman-style initiation into the secrets of the universe after you emerge from the phase of the Hanged Man.

In reverse, the Hanged Man signifies the inability to adjust to a new paradigm. Receiving this card in a reading could indicate that you're fighting progress, that you're playing the victim, or that you're not self-aware enough to handle the transitions ahead. Tune deeply into your thoughts and try to experiment by playing devil's advocate with yourself as much as possible. Turn your life on its head for a resolution to this issue.

13. Death

The Death card is not as literal as you might think, and I strongly

discourage you from feeling scared or frustrated when you draw this card! Death is one of the most inspiring and positive cards in the deck, as a matter of fact. Death signifies full-on transformation. One must submerge into the depths of the self before he or she can rise up with new power. Consider the images of the Phoenix, the resurrection, and the initiation. When you draw this card, it suggests that you may be about to greet your shadow side. But if you do, you'll be remade stronger, more powerful, and more passionate about your goals than ever before. Prepare for intensity, passion, and the shedding of what doesn't serve you.

In reverse, Death signifies that you're about to greet your shadow side, but

the outcome may not be as beneficial as you'd like unless you change a few things. For now, this card in reverse suggests that you're likely to meet your shadow with fear, which could lead to stagnation, exhaustion, and pessimism. As you move forward, stay open to what's to come and agree to forgive yourself to avoid the worst.

14. Temperance

The card of Temperance signifies potential for magic, lasting peace, and

pain transmuted into positivity. This card is a very hopeful one to draw in any reading. If you do draw Temperance, it likely means that you've just emerged from a period of great upheaval, or it could suggest that you have just come to incredible new knowledge about yourself in a spiritual sense. What you do with this enhanced knowledge is what can be likened to magic.

In reverse, Temperance signifies that you're in a state of imbalance. You've

lost track of your path and your center, and you may have been extra argumentative with others recently, too. You're likely feeling fragmented or torn in disparate directions, and you'll need to bring yourself back together before you can achieve any sense of harmony. Look to the surrounding cards to find out how to go about that.

15. The Devil

Despite its name, this card – like the Death card – appears more terrifying

than it actually is. Drawing this card does not mean you're possessed or doomed in any sense. It *can* mean, however, that you're being controlled by something external or material that you'd be better off free from. Consider how you're being repressed or obsessed by things outside yourself. Consider how you're being controlled or limited by some potential addiction (whether it be to drugs, alcohol, cigarettes, coffee, shopping, stealing, etc.). The Devil card points out how you've been shackled, and it reminds you how important it is to reclaim your own power of will.

In reverse, the Devil signifies what you likely feared from the Devil card itself: detrimental circumstances, abuse of power, devastating unhappiness, lack of self-control to temptation, and the (re)surfacing of one's inner demons. If you draw this card, be very cautious about how you proceed. If you aim for growth, many things will need to change.

16. The Tower

The Tower card suggests that you remained imprisoned by the Devil card and had to fight your way out. Traditionally, the Tower represents strife, conflict, destruction, devastation, and utter despair; however, I see the Tower as a bit more hopeful. If you draw the Tower, it means that you've decided to fight for something you believe in, and you're destroying everything left of that toxicity in order to succeed in your fight. The destruction comes from your liberation. The upheaval comes from immense and instant illumination. The beauty of creation awaits you once more as soon as your struggles settle.

In reverse, the Tower signifies that the concept of illumination may have been frightening or daunting to you. It suggests that you've shut yourself up in the tower, rather than broken free from it. Furthermore, concepts of imprisonment and avoidance of responsibility abound when pulling this card. If you do draw the Tower reversed in a reading, remember to release all fear and proceed as bravely and confidently as possible.

17. The Star

The Star card represents a beautiful and transcendent openness that

results from true illumination. This card suggests the happy resolution to all the events signified by the Tower. Furthermore, the Star contains the potential for wholeness, lasting healing, and completion of detrimental cycles. If you draw this card in your reading, be proud yet calm and hopeful! Good things are coming your way.

In reverse, the Star signifies what can happen when the Tower in reverse

advances in time: stagnation, waste of time, loss of self-respect, and loss of intuitive potential. If you shut yourself down to the potential for illumination, it's not surprising that you'll have likewise shut yourself down to progress and growth. Breathe deeply and believe in yourself as you move forward with this knowledge.

18. The Moon

The Moon card takes a step beyond what's happened with the Star and

asserts the querent as a fully-functioning psychic-in-training. If you draw this card, embrace the divine feminine in your life and devote yourself to your truth. Be unafraid to greet your shadow self, for your dark reflection is still that: *your reflection*. You may withdraw from society for a time (or you may be in that period now), but that withdrawal does not mean isolation, for you will be (or are) spiritually journeying the entire time. Keep an eye on your dreams and remember that your imagination can do incredible things.

In reverse, the Moon signifies a state of confusion brought about by being

unable to integrate your newfound faith or spirituality. If you draw this card, you likely feel uncomfortable with the concept or action of imagination. You may be relying on substances for your spiritual growth, too. There may have been signs pointing you in different directions, but you haven't followed them yet. To heal your current path, you'll need to proceed carefully. Look inside yourself for answers.

19. The Sun

The Sun card represents what the sun typically symbolizes: joy, freedom,

happiness, carefree energy, expansiveness, wonder, and success. Furthermore, this card suggests that you've begun to follow your path to enlightenment, and you're currently feeling the focus and clarity to fully achieve your dreams (as long as you stay on this path!). Remain optimistic and be unafraid to share what you've learned with others! Knowledge is light, after all.

In reverse, the Sun signifies that your inner light has dimmed. Perhaps you've refused to share your knowledge with others. Perhaps you're unable to see things clearly. Perhaps you're arrogant and assume you don't need to know more. Whatever your circumstances are, you doubt yourself or your path to some degree, and it's negatively affecting your psyche. However, this card could simply suggest that the success you crave is merely delayed.

20. Judgment

The card of Judgment is another card of rebirth. It insists that there will be

a whole new set of paths to follow after you're settled in that energy of the Sun card. When one door closes, so many more open. Judgment also signifies that a time for decision-making is at hand. There are many changes ahead, and you'll be tested to see if you can carry your frequency of light. Make the decisions that best reflect your truth in order to succeed.

In reverse, Judgment signifies that you've heard the call to act, to change, and to become reborn, but the trouble is that you've ignored it. You may not be ready to understand what's at hand, but you could also just be willfully ignorant. If you pull this card, consider how you may be acting out of a fear of change.

21. The World

The World card is another in the tarot that symbolizes completion. Those who draw this card have gone through periods of great success that brought lasting satisfaction and pride. The World card is about celebration. It's about the dancing done when you've achieved all that you hoped for. It's about the festivities – the union of self and world – that occur when one's in his or her prime. The World demonstrates that abundance (if not currently achieved) is nearer than you think! Keep your chin up and be patient. You won't have to wait much longer.

In reverse, the World signifies delay of success. There may be limitations in place, or you could feel like you're in a state of suspended animation. If you're feeling anything but validated and free, it's likely that your most important work is not completed quite yet. If this card is pulled, I recommend waiting out the situation, for movement and progress will absolutely return in time.

22. (0.) The Fool

The Fool both opens and closes the Major Arcana, and that's because it associates most strongly with innocence, openness, and new beginnings. The Fool represents both closure and conception. It's a card of balanced extremes and energy focused through playfulness. If you've drawn the Fool, it could be because you're acting like one, but it could also be because you need to take a less serious route in life in order to succeed. Remember to laugh at yourself! Take yourself less seriously and play a little more! Optimism comes to those who maintain good humor.

In reverse, the Fool signifies that you're playing out the worst qualities of the card. You're childlike, playful, and extreme, yes. But you're also naïve, irrational, and foolhardy. Don't be afraid of change! Don't let yourself be trapped by routine either! You may be naïve and gullible now, but your awareness of these traits is pivotal knowledge to be able to change them in the future.

Minor Arcana

The Minor Arcana, also called the Lesser Arcana, represents personality aspects and struggles or experiences that exist for all humanity in this world. The Minor Arcana is divided into 16 court or face cards and 40 "pip" or numbered cards from ace to 10. These 56 cards are all also divided into 4 suits or elemental types. Sometimes the suits are called different things, but I've noted where that terminology may differ for your convenience.

Wands (a.k.a. – Clubs / Batons / Staves)

Wands, Clubs, Batons, and Staves all represent the same energy. This suit is all about passion, inspiration, initiation, impulsiveness, action, physical sensation, and strength-building. Wands often signify what is generated in order to inspire others. Furthermore, they're associated with summertime.

Ace of Wands

The Ace of Wands is all about birth, new action, and expression of creative energy. Those who draw this card are unerringly gifted with a creative energy of some type, and they're likely to have the vigor to express that gift soon (if they haven't already). Sometimes, this card also represents recent conception or the upcoming birth of a child.

In reverse, this card signifies that there's a blockage in your energy, creative or otherwise. As long as you're aware of this blockage, it's soon to pass.

2 of Wands

The 2 of Wands symbolizes a tension that may be blocking that free-flow of creativity. How do you feel about your work? Are you truly satisfied in your life? This card encourages you to examine what might be holding you back. Once you figure out what it is, you will have established a doorway that will change your circumstances once it is opened.

In reverse, this card signifies a sudden release of tension which can translate into a creative work of genius.

3 of Wands

The 3 of Wands shows you how hard you've been working. You probably didn't need the confirmation, but your higher self wants you to know that he or she has noticed all the effort you've been putting in. Rewards are coming, and a whole new path may be revealed in a short time. Maintain confidence and direction for your goals are within reach!

In reverse, this card signifies that you may have been following a dream that's just not right for you – at least not right now. Think deeply about your goals and see if you can find the one that's misaligned from your truth. Another meaning of this card in reverse is that you've been focusing too much on the past in order to move into your own future.

4 of Wands

The 4 of Wands shows that the effort you've put into building a happy home has paid off. Things are feeling supportive, stabilized, comforting, and rewarding. You have a sense that you're settled enough with your life and your family to start the major project you've been putting off for so long. You're proud, joyful, and ready for what the world has in store.

In reverse, this card signifies much of the same as the right-side-up version. The only difference is that you may have a temporary break from your work that's caused by a delay in action. If you experience this break, take full advantage of it. Rest up for what's to come.

5 of Wands

The 5 of Wands symbolizes playful conflict on the horizon. There's an interplay of activities and minds that's been surrounding you, but there may be an interruption to – or heightening of – that energy soon. Stand firm in your truth and open yourself up to the possibility for a sexual liaison (if you're into it!) because it could be the right time with that special someone.

In reverse, this card signifies conflict experienced internally. There could also be a degree of mistrust against oneself that's been holding you back. Turn to meditation to reestablish your trust in yourself and look to the surrounding cards in your spread to receive clues about the situation as a whole.

6 of Wands

The 6 of Wands represents recent victory achieved through focused and sustained effort. It demonstrates that you have the capacity to be a leader (once you're ready to embrace that role). Furthermore, the 6 of Wands reveals your potential for fame. Any actions you undertake towards your goal will end up successful as long as this card is in play.

In reverse, this card signifies how disastrous distrust can be. It can derail you from your path, it can shut off connections to others, and it can eliminate potential positions. If you've let distrust infect your heart and mind, it's time to work for resolution. On the other hand, if you see distrust creeping into your life right now, try to get to the root of the issue and eradicate it before it gets stuck in you for good.

7 of Wands

The 7 of Wands reveals struggles on your horizon. There may be challenges to your authority that you don't appreciate, or it could just be that you're not feeling properly respected in your line of work. If you draw this card, proceed with caution and try to discern the biggest obstacles in your life through meditation. Once they're discovered, you can process these obstacles yourself without bringing the issue to others (and that would just make matters so much worse anyway).

In reverse, this card signifies that you're feeling some emotional turmoil over your work situation. Maybe someone has criticized your work, and you're frustrated or embarrassed. Maybe someone has told you the boss is checking on your work and you're extra stressed. Regardless of the situation, try not to let other peoples' concerns weigh you down. Work to your highest capacity and remember to live your truth if you're ready to settle this imbalance.

8 of Wands

The 8 of Wands card is all about speed, accuracy, and aim. This card signals that you're like an arrow shot expertly toward its target. You're swiftly approaching all you hope for so strongly, and anything you attempt at this time is bound to be efficient, successful, serendipitous, and exciting. Don't get caught up in the vibe! Try to use this energy for actualization and action.

In reverse, this card signifies that something is ending for you. Feelings of foreboding, concern, and frustration abound for you right now, and you fear losing things (and people) that mean the most to you. In order to succeed and not flounder, it may be difficult, but all it takes is an attitude check to shift things in the right direction.

9 of Wands

The 9 of Wands symbolizes a moment of lull for you. You've just been through some nonsense, and the conflict is still playing out in your heart and mind. Because of this recent conflict and any lingering tensions, you may be feeling fearful or unsure of your future. You may be more antisocial or shy than ever, and it's unlikely that you're willing to take on big, life-altering action.

However, this card encourages you to go for it! Let go of the pain and dive back into the experience! You never know what beautiful outcomes will arise.

In reverse, this card signifies that you're intensely working away at an internal issue. Whatever you've noticed within yourself that you don't like, you've decided to eradicate it. However, the issue is a bit more ingrained in you than you initially thought! Have hope and be stubborn! Try a different approach to the situation! If that doesn't work, the surrounding cards in this reading may provide the clues you need for resolution.

10 of Wands

The 10 of Wands focuses on feelings of overwork. You've put a lot of effort into your vocation or a project of choice, and you're desperate to start seeing rewards. If you work for someone else, it could be that they're asking too much of you. If you are self-employed, it could be that you're tackling too much. Be careful not to burn yourself out, but know that if you do, another path to success will emerge to direct you in time.

In reverse, this card signifies the potential for freedom. It could be that a new path is opening up for you, but it could also be that an old path is burning and crumbling before your eyes. Keep an eye open for clues in your life that can direct you to this liberating path. Over time, you will achieve balance and just reward.

Page of Wands

The Page of Wands insists that a young and energetic person may be about to enter your life. This person will provide needed inspiration to your life, and he or she may signify a new phase of your own life about to begin. Things are about to pick up for you!

In reverse, this card signifies that someone who's overly confused or uncertain may enter your life instead. You may need to serve as an example for them so that you both aren't distracted to the point of stagnation. Remember to remain energetic and resolute despite this (person's) energy.

Knight of Wands

The Knight of Wands reminds you of the passion and eagerness that can accompany pure and fresh ideas. You might have been feeling listless or directionless lately, but that's all about to change. It could be a person that inspires you or a philosophy or a course of action. Whatever it is, it will provide challenges that help you grow exponentially. All you needed was a little bit of rebellious information to inspire you!

In reverse, this card signifies that you lack the energy you need to either act or think appropriately. As much as possible, be sure not to lie, not to lose your temper, not to control people, and not to ignore your passions. It's time to live authentically and fruitfully!

Queen of Wands

The Queen of Wands suggests that a wise, generous, and creative feminine presence is about to enter your life. It can mean that you're about to channel this energy for yourself, too. Don't shy away from femininity, charity, altruism, or compassion at this time! Be brave and express your willingness to help others. Volunteerism is a great practice at this time.

In reverse, this card signifies that you, someone else, or your mentality are about to take away from the freedoms of others. Make sure that your goals don't detract from the lives of others when you pull this card. Double-check your intentions, too. It can't hurt to reexamine them once in a while regardless.

King of Wands

The King of Wands symbolizes a person, opinion, or philosophy that's perfected through effort and hardened through passion. In your life, this card could represent troubling or stressful negotiations with others. Furthermore, it could signify a financial settlement that's about to be decided in your favor. Finally, the King of Wands suggests that it's time to take up the limelight and own your hard-earned successes.

In reverse, this card signifies that the hopefulness, direction, eagerness, enthusiasm, passion, and intensity of the King of Wands has been focused toward either extreme positive or extreme negative expression. Don't let other people tear you down, but don't do that same thing to others either! This card teaches the value of love and sacrifice in protection and progress, respectively.

Swords

Swords are all about intellect, mentalism, thoughtfulness, analytical thinking, concrete planning, and even deceitful scheming. Swords often signify what is sensed intuitively and then developed intellectually. They are also associated with springtime.

Ace of Swords

The Ace of Swords represents mental clarity as well as success on the horizon. It suggests that you've been given a gift of intellect, and it encourages you to use that gift to the advantage of all others. There are incredible opportunities available to you in your field as long as you show confidence in yourself and your craft.

In reverse, this card signifies that you're experiencing imbalance or harshness on your journey related to overreliance on judgment. Remember that others are a reflection of you and that separation is an illusion in order to reestablish balance.

2 of Swords

The 2 of Swords predicts an opposition in your future. Whether it's between you and someone else or between two other people, there's conflict and strife ahead. You may be asked to be the mediator if you're not too personally involved in the situation. If you draw this card, double-check yourself to be sure not to put off your responsibilities to others.

In reverse, this card signifies internal conflict, tension, and self-deceit. Devote yourself to your truth in order to change the situation.

3 of Swords

The 3 of Swords isn't the most positive card to pull. It represents a time of great heartache. It could be that you've recently experienced a breakup, or you might just be in a phase of personal transformation. Regardless of the reason, your heart is torn apart by some sort of conflict. Let these emotions fill you and don't avoid them – they will help you grow in ways you could never imagine (at least, not right now).

In reverse, this card signifies that an old wound may be re-opened soon. It may already be raw and re-opened right now. Allow yourself to forgive whoever wronged you, and don't let yourself get caught up in feelings of woundedness or victimhood. Take the high road.

4 of Swords

The 4 of Swords represents the importance of discernment. You may be about to face (or you're currently facing) an intense conflict, and you'll need to make sure you confront those who deserve it while retreating from others who don't. You'll need to make sure that you're aligned with your stable foundation of truth in order to stay above the struggles. Meditation may help you be able to keep the peace.

In reverse, this card signifies that you're ready to come back into the world after a period of isolation. You've been hurt, but you're healing, so you emerge armed with positive energy for the future.

5 of Swords

The 5 of Swords warns you that you're coming up against hardship. There will be struggle ahead, and you may not turn out to be the victor. There may be threats to your dignity or failures in tests of loyalty. There may be a breakdown of communication between friends or lovers that proves toxic, and you'll have to remain open and willing to improve in order to find closure with this issue.

In reverse, this card signifies feelings of despair that fill you. These feelings have surfaced due to a defeat you recently suffered. Allow yourself to be forgiven, and instead of wallowing, follow the path to renewal.

6 of Swords

The 6 of Swords shares important information about peace. It reveals that peace can come from the sharing of differences with others. Truth is not consistent. It is subjective, individual, and largely underappreciated, which is why it's so important for each of us to share our truths with others. This sharing increases the collective capacity for empathy, understanding, and growth. By drawing this card, you've shown that you're ready to move beyond separation from others to a place of intellectual solidarity that's achieved through appreciation of difference.

In reverse, this card signifies the pain you sense in confrontation. Sometimes, confrontation is so painful that we put it off for months, if not years. Sometimes, confrontation is so overwhelming that you get stuck and refuse to process the pain behind the circumstance. Pulling this card means that you must face the issue or resolve it within yourself in order to move forward.

7 of Swords

The 7 of Swords is a card to be very excited about! It suggests that magical knowledge is just past your fingertips. You may be about to embark on a voyage of great learning – or it could be that your spirit guides are about to "take you to school" to relearn your basics before growth can be achieved. Regardless, there's a definite air of excitement in your life, and new veins of knowledge shine out to you in the darkness.

In reverse, this card signifies a number of things. It could be that you're about to help someone out, rework a previous conflict, receive previously stolen goods, use your words against someone, or experience intense trickery or deception. Regardless, things are about to get weird, and the essence of mystery stands firm throughout any upcoming struggles.

8 of Swords

The 8 of Swords represents a tricky situation that you likely feel stuck in. Whether it's due to your circumstances or the needs of another person, you're restricted, tied down, and focused on thinking through fear. Try to remember that fear is just a mindset (and an unproductive one, at that!). Focus instead on using your mind to establish your own liberation, and you should be able to find the silver lining to the situation in no time.

In reverse, this card signifies that a time of escape or entrapment is almost over for you. You see freedom on the horizon, and you're willing to do anything to achieve that freedom. Ignore gossip and drama that wants to stand in your way, and then you're sure to succeed.

9 of Swords

The 9 of Swords represents that you may be deep in a period of darkness, internally. Although things may look alright on the outside, on the inside, you're experiencing anguish, despair, and utter devastation. You could be experiencing the powerful and formative moment that many call the "Dark Night of the Soul." Remember that you're not as alone as you think you are and keep your sights on your goals! Don't lose track of your truth in this state, for the outcome can be an identity crisis.

In reverse, this card signifies one of two things. First, it could be that your truth is being used against your will in ways you're uncomfortable with (i.e., as a scapegoat for blame or as an avatar for someone's ethnic or religious hatred). Second, it could be that troubling situations are about to get much better. Either way, expect blunt realizations and potential for deep transformations.

10 of Swords

The 10 of Swords represents the lowest point you can reach, but it also realizes that the lowest lows occur right before the brightest dawns. If you're feeling dejected, misdirected, undervalued, inferior, or betrayed right now, know that things *will* be okay in time. Things may end for you on the short-term, but that will open up avenues for success in the long-term. Remember that things tend to happen in 3s and proceed with as little hatred as possible.

In reverse, this card signifies that you've made a deep and lasting realization recently regarding your perceptions of life. You used to think things unfair or unbalanced or frustrating, but you've just accepted that you have the power to change your reality. Look inside and heal conflicts on that level to see what reverberates into more external realms.

Page of Swords

The Page of Swords could represent you (or someone else) who's having trouble with communication. New lessons for this person are about to arise, but he or she will have to practice in order to establish fluency and eloquence. It could also be that incredible conversations are coming your way! Don't be afraid to start up a discussion with a stranger.

In reverse, this card signifies that you (or someone near you) is being too detached in life. Get close to others and be unafraid of forming bonds! However, be careful not to become too controlling of others at this time.

Knight of Swords

The Knight of Swords is all about revolutionary intelligence. You may be about to meet a person or encounter a theory or philosophy that's completely radical. It (or he/she) will challenge everything you thought you knew, and you'll emerge smarter and stronger. You may be about to embark on travel through the air.

In reverse, this card signifies that you're approaching something in the wrong way. Whether it's a person, a thing, or a situation, you're just not coming at it quite right. Be selfless and reject urges for control, aggression, or abuse whenever they arise.

Queen of Swords

The Queen of Swords reveals the presence of someone feminine who's devoted to justice. This person may be about to enter your life, or it could be you who's about to step up to the plate. Furthermore, this card can simply signal a shift of attitude from subjectivity to objectivity for the sake of the greater good.

In reverse, this card signifies a feminine energy that's devoted to justice but who's suffered greatly at the hands of the system. Pulling this card can mean that you, your philosophy on life, or someone else close to you has become embittered to the point of detachment from social spheres. Bitterness is a disease that can be cured by connection with others, so fight this frustration with love!

King of Swords

The King of Swords is all about legal, medical, scientific, or financial advancement. It could represent a person high-up in any one of these fields, but it could also suggest that you hold this potential with yourself. When you pull this card, look to the areas in *your* own life that could use a better foundation. Especially be wary of unsteady backgrounds in terms of justice, self-sufficiency, honesty, and intellect.

In reverse, this card signifies that even the purest goals can be twisted with impure intention. It reminds you to check your strategy so that you're not hurting anyone, intentionally or not. Furthermore, this card encourages you to communicate your truth *tactfully* to others. Otherwise, you may come up against intense and long-lasting conflict over your word choice.

Cups (a.k.a. – Chalices)

Cups and Chalices both represent the same energy. This suit is about emotionality, the sensual world, creativity and growth, and wateriness. Cups often signify what is felt deeply and encouraged toward others. Furthermore, they're associated with autumnal times of the year.

Ace of Cups

The Ace of Cups symbolizes the blossoming of romantic intention. Essentially, it reveals the potential for new emotional interests related to creation, inspiration, or romance. There are new relationships of all sorts on the horizon, or it could be that your relationship with something or someone is about to be kicked up a notch.

In reverse, this card signifies that you're experiencing a lull in romance or creative inspiration. If you find yourself drawing this card, ask yourself what you may have recently rejected that would have actually served you well.

2 of Cups

The 2 of Cups demonstrates prosperous and amorous times ahead! Those seeking romance or healing will find their wishes fulfilled, and those seeking reconciliation with others will also find their hopes confirmed. The 2 of Cups reveals how love can be a powerful force for healing in so many ways.

In reverse, this card signifies pain induced from love gone awry. Your emotions are intense, and they can drag you down into your own depths, but rest easy knowing that satisfaction *will* come into your life again.

3 of Cups

The 3 of Cups symbolizes a lively, celebratory time filled with glee, love, and togetherness. This card represents shared joy over gifts that will benefit the community. You may have just made it through a troubling time, or it may be time to harvest the fruits of your hard work. Regardless of the cause, give yourself to the revelry! Treat yourself! You deserve it.

In reverse, this card signifies the worst aspects of a life filled with partying: overindulgence, overspending, and superficiality. Make sure you satisfy your inner needs as well as your external ones in order to correct this imbalance.

4 of Cups

The 4 of Cups represents a period in which your emotions or your daily "flow" feel out of balance or interrupted. You may have overworked yourself recently, which could be causing this imbalance. It could also be that your best friendships and/or your partnership feel off-kilter, making everything else out of whack. If you're feeling stagnant or indifferent, try to bask in the comforts that surround you. Positivity is the trick to escaping this mood.

In reverse, this card signifies that you're ready to move on from this period of stagnation and indifference! Your energy has been redirected, and after all you've been through, you're ready to once again take on the world.

5 of Cups

The 5 of Cups represents a complication added to your standard emotional satisfaction. You likely weren't expecting this complication, and you're unsure how to respond to it. Feelings of abandonment, surprise, fear, worthlessness, and loss arise, but you know that they're not the norm for you. You could be holding on to the past too harshly. Look to the present and future in order to heal this wound.

In reverse, this card signifies that you've suffered immensely, but you've reached the perfect time to move forward. It's a great time to resolve unfinished business with others or to reassess a conflict from the past. Keep an open heart and remember the value of mercy.

6 of Cups

The 6 of Cups symbolizes (re)union, gatherings, and exchanges. This card reveals the importance of love across time and space, for you may be about to reunite with unknown family, old friends, previous lovers, or embittered rivals from the past. It's time to rehash those old relationships and find out how they helped you grow (even if it didn't feel like growth at the time).

In reverse, this card signifies trials involved with revisiting one's past. You may find that wounds you thought had healed are actually still quite raw. You might find that reunion experiences don't end up as productive as you'd hoped. If you draw this card, take things slowly, and don't put yourself through too much emotional stress anytime soon.

7 of Cups

The 7 of Cups suggests that you have a lot on your mind. Numerous goals and dreams are competing for focus in your head, and therefore, no path rings true, and no dreams feel 100% worth following. Be patient throughout this period of scattered energy, for focus will return in time. For the time being, entertain all these possible dreams and play them out in your head (rather than in real life) to see how realistic they actually are.

In reverse, this card signifies that you've delayed your decision-making either too long or exactly the right amount of time. Therefore, this card could represent a missed opportunity, or it could suggest that you're right on schedule, using your will power to achieve your goals with perfection.

8 of Cups

The 8 of Cups suggests that it might be time for you to move on. You've dedicated a lot of your energy recently (or over the past few years) to a relationship that's become unproductive. Don't ignore that truth anymore: things are now utterly and unavoidably *unproductive*. It's time to step away. It's time to move on, and that may seem harsh, but I promise that new growth will replace what you've lost.

In reverse, this card signifies that you're going through a rough point in your current romantic relationship. You're considering the pros and cons, and you're thinking of what it would be like to be single (or with someone else) again. You may be thinking this so often that you're exhausted of it by now. It's not likely that action will result from these thoughts at this time.

9 of Cups

The 9 of Cups signifies that something you've worked very hard to attain is finally within grasp. It represents satisfaction, contentment, and deep and lasting happiness. The 9 of Cups also suggests that any conflicts that arise around this time will be easily defused. Finally, this card represents the potential for laziness and stagnation if you wallow in this success for too long without establishing a new path. As always, the ending of one thing must correlate to the beginning of another. Keep your efforts focused on that next up-swing.

In reverse, this card signifies how something that used to stand in your way is now resolved. Whether it was yourself, something, or someone else, whatever was holding you back is just about conquered. Make sure you're not overindulging during this time, as it can hinder your ability to finalize this conquest.

10 of Cups

The 10 of Cups symbolizes emotional fulfillment. Everything you hoped for yourself now feels within reach, and you're brimming with love for both yourself and others. This card is extremely hopeful, as it encourages you to reach for the stars. In success-filled moments, don't forget to keep dreaming! This card will remind you of what's possible when you think you've achieved all your wishes.

In reverse, this card signifies that there may be struggles at home. Whether it's with your family or your intimate partner, things are decidedly rocky. It could be that someone's leaving home, and you're having trouble adjusting. Keep an open heart and embrace the change that you face rather than fighting it. It may seem unfathomable, but you will adjust in time.

Page of Cups

The Page of Cups demonstrates a new direction for creativity. You might be starting a new artistic venture, or you may be about to bring a baby into this world! New things are starting up everywhere, and you'll have to make sure your cup is brimming with love if you plan to take it all in.

In reverse, this card signifies hardship associated with love or creative direction. You may have all the urge to succeed, but your emotions or actions could disagree. It could be that you're confused about what you actually need from your art, from yourself, from your job, and/or from others. Start meditating to find the answer or look to the surrounding cards for clues.

Knight of Cups

The Knight of Cups represents either a person or an attitude that's idealistic, hopeful, romantic, and dreamy. Be careful not to be too naïve in your dreams and ideals, however, for some things are not as easy to manifest as you'd think. You might be about to use your healing abilities to help others, but you also might be about to engage in travel over water. This card has many meanings.

In reverse, this card signifies that something (or someone) is hiding from you in plain sight. Be true to yourself, and make sure you're not the one hiding! Bring your secrets out of the darkness, and clean any skeletons out of your closet. It's time for some emotional spring-cleaning if you're hoping for growth.

Queen of Cups

The Queen of Cups symbolizes a person in your life who is truly devoted to loving you. This person is likely *not* your partner. More often than not, it's a teacher, a parent, a guardian, or a therapist (regardless of gender) whose interactions with you are more nurturing than anything else. This person will be of increasing importance to you in the near future. This card can also suggest that your creative dreams are about to be actualized.

In reverse, this card signifies one's struggles to feel comfortable in a new social setting. Things have changed recently, but you're not adjusting well. You're unsure, guarded, alienated, and uncomfortable. Try to channel happiness often, and work on healing your deepest emotional wounds in order to correct this imbalance.

King of Cups

The King of Cups demonstrates that a sensitive, spiritual, and emotional masculine person may be about to enter your life, but it can also suggest that a new spiritual (or artistic) path is about to be revealed to you instead. Look out for jobs (or people interested) in the fields of publishing, music, art, or theatre.

In reverse, this card signifies that your partner (or potential partner) is too distracted to be able to love you (or him or herself) fully. It could be that he or she is caught off-guard by the relationship, but it's more likely that it's a substance abuse issue. This card is both a warning and an opportunity for transformation.

Pentacles (a.k.a. – Coins / Rings / Discs)

Pentacles, Coins, Rings, and Discs all represent the same energy. This suit is all about materialism, home life, and earthiness. Pentacles often signify what is realized and then put into action. Furthermore, they're associated with wintery times of the year.

Ace of Pentacles

The Ace of Pentacles suggests that financial gain is on your horizon! There is a hint of something prosperous starting up for you soon. Furthermore, you may feel a sense of deep peace at this time with respect to your job, your relationships, and your home life. However, it could be that only *one* of these aspects of your life evokes this serene sensation.

In reverse, this card signifies how you may be controlled by vice. Greed, lust, addiction, envy, and sloth are most likely to be the vice in question. Let go of any unnecessary attachments in order to heal this issue.

2 of Pentacles

The 2 of Pentacles symbolizes the need for trust in upcoming trying times. You may feel instinctually that you should proceed with caution, but that urge is not actually the best option for you right now. Open yourself to the universe and to the possibilities that others will offer. Find a balance between intellect and play, and remember to trust in the process.

In reverse, this card signifies that what you're trying to balance or juggle isn't exactly working out. You risk losing money and resources if you follow the path you've been on. Proceed with caution.

3 of Pentacles

The 3 of Pentacles shows you how you've actualized the fruits of your labor! All that you've been working on will soon be finalized, and you'll receive all the necessary compensation and praise shortly, so be patient! If you have the sense to improve the work you've done, follow that intuition! It will likely develop your project to an even more advanced (and prosperous) level.

In reverse, this card signifies that laziness (or fear) has gotten in the way of your success. Your projects stand incomplete due to self-doubt or procrastination. If you feel something's (or some*one*'s) been undermining you, try to find the source of that issue so that you can realize the fruits of your labor in time.

4 of Pentacles

The 4 of Pentacles signifies a foundation being built in material possessions or wealth. Your hard work is certainly paying off, and you may be well on your way to building an empire from that work.

However, make sure you don't become too detached from people and emotions with all this focus on finances and work!

In reverse, this card signifies that it's finally time to open up and release the emotional burdens you've been holding on to for so long. You may have been making a storehouse of "unproductive" emotions, and now is the perfect time to face that storehouse head on, so you can heal and actually move forward.

5 of Pentacles

The 5 of Pentacles represents financial bereavements. Unexpected loss recently slapped you in the face (or it soon will!), so you're feeling undermined, underwhelmed, disappointed, and disillusioned. Don't let this pain break you down completely, for material goods can be regained. Re-examine your life to see what other types of abundance you may have been overlooking in order to heal this wound.

In reverse, this card signifies a turning point of sorts. It may not be financial, and it's more than likely relationship-based instead. This turning point has been signaled to you through your intense desire to recreate failed emotional intimacies with new people. Allow these new (relationship) foundations to be structured from the ruins of what others have left behind. Transform that negativity into something more productive!

6 of Pentacles

The 6 of Pentacles symbolizes that you can't receive abundance in a vacuum–you have to put goodness and abundance out into the world in order to receive it for yourself. This card, therefore, encourages individuals to channel generosity with others as much as possible. The more selfless you can become, the more the universe will be able to recognize your goodness, and then it will provide for you in kind.

In reverse, this card signifies struggles with money as well as debt to others. You may be working through selfishness–or you may be attempting more caution– when it comes to money. Anything you can do to become selfless and generous will help you cure this imbalance. And once the imbalance is cured, the universe will send blessings your way too.

7 of Pentacles

The 7 of Pentacles reveals that it's time to harvest the fruits of your relationships! Whether professional, personal, or romantic, your relationships will be especially abundant at this point, and you'll likely learn a good number of lessons in terms of relating to others at this time. Don't worry about interfering with things in your life in order to affirm any future growth, for it will happen to you without any effort on your part. You are aligned with success, and the only thing you can do to help is to clean out any (emotional, physical, or spiritual) clutter that remains.

In reverse, this card signifies that your life, your work, and/or your relationships are not currently satisfying. They're not only dissatisfying; they're also energetically *frustrating*. If you feel things are unfair or unequal in these realms right now, don't let patience or exhaustion stand in the way of you expressing your truth.

8 of Pentacles

The 8 of Pentacles is a card focused on patience. This card recognizes that you currently have huge goals and that you've been putting in a lot of hard work. It sees your successes and hardships, and it wants you to succeed even further, but just know that this outcome will require even *more* hard work. Work like a turtle (slow and steady) until your end-goals are settled firmly in sight! It could be that you're about to enter an internship or apprenticeship that realigns your direction entirely, too.

In reverse, this card signifies that you're hoping for success without any work to support these hopes. You've got grand dreams, but you're physically lazy. There's a disjunction–an imbalance–between theory and application, and you won't truly become established and prolific until you correct these imbalances. You might be in the wrong vocational field entirely, as a matter of fact!

9 of Pentacles

The 9 of Pentacles represents all that success will establish in your life once you have it. You will experience an abundance of all sorts, and you will have new pleasures to experience with others you trust. Furthermore, this card suggests that you will only be able to establish that success once your environment matches your values. It could be that a change of vocation is in order, so that you can work in alignment with your ethics.

In reverse, this card signifies that you are lost from the path you worked so hard to find. It could be that you haven't found your path at all, and the weight of that truth weighs on you. It could be, on the other hand, that you're unable to accept the responsibility necessary to succeed in this manner. Relocate your priorities, and get back in touch with discipline to balance out this issue.

10 of Pentacles

The 10 of Pentacles focuses on what's called an attitude of gratitude, or a mindset of abundance. When you pull the 10 of Pentacles, your higher self is telling you to wake up and realize your blessings! There are likely far more than you've recently noticed. Feel the weight of these blessings in your life, express gratitude often, and accept that your mindset attracts abundance. If you're working to attract abundance of this nature without success, don't fret. This card reminds you that outcomes are sometimes delayed in order to teach a message. For you, this time the message is likely: be patient.

In reverse, this card signifies that the bonds of family are either troubling or unproductive to you at the current moment. It may help you to see a distinction between "Earth family" and "chosen family." Embrace your friends, your pets, and your close colleagues as kin, and allow yourself to detach from and release the pressures put on you by any troubling Earth family members. You owe them nothing, especially if they don't appreciate you.

Page of Pentacles

The Page of Pentacles insists that a new (and profitable!) phase of your life is about to begin. Especially at this time, take note of any ideas that enter your head! They are likely to be the intellectual seeds of your future business or other high-achieving projects.

In reverse, this card signifies that you've been working too hard for something that's just an idea (at this point, at least). Don't overextend yourself for a project that's far from completion. Work some, plan some, and relax some! That last step is crucial for your mental and physical health.

Knight of Pentacles

The Knight of Pentacles represents a practical and supportive person (or approach) that's about to impact your life intensely. Your goals for the immediate future likely involve getting back in touch with health through a new (or new-to-you) dietary or fitness practice. This card can also mean that a journey over land will be undertaken soon.

In reverse, this card signifies a person (or attitude) that's overly focused on material abundance to the detriment of spiritual, emotional, and mental practices of betterment. Don't forget to focus on healing and affirming your whole self, rather than just parts of yourself! Furthermore, this card can represent inner turmoil being turned into positivity in a variety of ways.

Queen of Pentacles

The Queen of Pentacles represents a person (or attitude) that needs to devote more care to one's body, one's land, one's possessions, one's financial estate, and/or one's relationships. This question asks the querent what he or she is doing to support the land we come from. Furthermore, this card can represent the need to treat yourself if times have been hard.

In reverse, this card signifies an unfortunate internal state during which you may not recognize, trust, or support yourself, your instincts, and your dreams. Get back outside and in touch with nature if you're feeling this disassociation occurring. You can also recalibrate these feelings about yourself by getting back in touch with your animal self. Let go of what you're hoarding and donate material goods that don't serve you. Skim down on *things* to find yourself again.

King of Pentacles

The King of Pentacles is all about seeking (and achieving) improvement to one's financial situation. You've been working long and hard, and those efforts are about to pay off if they haven't already. Your own potential for traditional success (artistically or professionally) lies right under your nose.

In reverse, this card signifies the worst that high-achieving earthy energy has to offer. Essentially, it suggests stubbornness, rigidity, disrespectfulness, condescension, vulgarity, jealousy, and general inadequacy (pridefully posing as success). Keep an eye out for this problematic energy in your life.

Memorization Tricks

This section devotes its focus to establishing and explaining 5 different tricks you can use make memorizing all the meanings in the tarot a little easier. There are hidden patterns and meanings in the deck that you only need to know so that things will be immensely simpler. Check in with the tricks below to learn more!

Trick #1 – The Story in the Major Arcana

If you're having a hard time remembering the order of the Major Arcana, this trick may help you a lot. Similarly, if you're struggling to remember the *meanings* of the Major

Arcana cards, this trick will be equally helpful. There is a story about the history of humanity that's told in these first 22 cards, and once you know that story and its progressions, you may have a much easier time with your understanding of your own deck. The story follows this basic path:

At first, humankind emerged from the UNKNOWN (The Fool, #0). Then these bumbling humans realized the strength of their WILL (The Magician, #1) to change their circumstances, the importance of INTUITION (The High Priestess, #2) to tell what's true, the value of CREATIVITY (The Empress, #3) to populate the world, and the trickiness of REASON (The Emperor, #4), being that it's so important yet so hard to fully attain. TRADITION (The Hierophant, #5) taught these humans what had value, but CHOICE (The Lover, #6) gave them the ability to select what they wanted for themselves. Humans rose up TRIUMPHANT (The Chariot, #7) with their freedoms and felt DETERMINED (Strength, #8) to take on the ever-expanding world. However, with all these successes, humanity became INTROSPECTIVE (The Hermit, #9) regarding all those choices and paths not taken. Humanity felt the true weight of all the passing CHANGES (The Wheel of Fortune, #10) in their surrounding world and felt the need for true BALANCE (Justice, #11). With this urge for balance, however, there was a need for SACRIFICE (The Hanged Man, #12) and ENDINGS (Death, #13) of what no longer served the population. In the end, a BLENDING (Temperance, #14) of cultures and temperaments was achieved to the benefit of all. MATERIAL THINGS (The Devil, #15) increased, along with their destructive forces, while our DEEP INSIGHTS (The Tower, #16) into those losses were often ignored. Still, some humans had HOPE (The Star, #17), while others were stuck in the same DELUSIONS and ILLUSIONS (The Moon, #18) that things didn't need to change anymore.

Eventually, the truth was ILLUMINATED (The Sun, #19) for all to see, and great AWAKENINGS (Judgment, #20) spread across the land. Spirituality woke up in the population, giving them the truest GIFT (The World, #21) of existence. Ultimately, new humans were born with fresh INNOCENCE (The Fool, #22), despite their ancestors' wrongs, continuing this cycle into the future.

Trick #2 – The Elements in the Suits

A great trick for remembering the meaning of each suit in the Minor Arcana is to associate a natural element with each one. Wands are associated with fire, Cups are linked with water, Pentacles signify earth, and Swords are tied to air. Elementally, that means that Wands are linked with initiatory energy, adventure, travel, passions, and action, so any wand card you draw will have this energy deeply infused into it. Cups are linked with emotionality, deep feeling, introspection, healing, and curiosity, so any Cups you pull will have this associated energy. Pentacles are therefore associated with groundedness, home life, domesticity, earth-work, gardening, material goods, and financial prospects, so any Pentacles you draw will have this essential energy. Finally, Swords are linked with intellectual exploration, mental capacities, socialness, educational development, and the mind itself, so any Swords you draw in a reading will relate to this type of focus.

Trick #3 – The Meaning in the Numbers

While this association will be explained fully in Chapter 6, for now, it will suffice to say that the numbers on each card mean more than just their successive order in the series. Numbers contain intense power and significance, and if you can understand what the numbers on each card signify, you will have a much easier time memorizing both the Major and Minor Arcana.

Trick #4 – The Court / Face Cards

Within the Minor Arcana, 16-20 cards can be worked with individually in order for an easier time with memorization. These cards are the Court or Face cards. Often called Page, Knight, Queen, King, (and Ace) these cards *can* have different names, such as Princess, Prince, etc. Consult your deck for more specifics to see what the author decided to call them.

Essentially, each of these face cards represents a different phase of the individual's self-expression. While the Major Arcana discuss the inner mysteries of humanity as a whole and its journey across time to today, the Minor Arcana talks more about individual people, traits, and experiences that come to shape each person's self-expression in this lifetime.

Whenever you see a Page, know that the energy is focused on inexperienced energy that aches for self-expression. Pages in Cups and Pentacles represent feminine energy of the goddess, slowness, and receptivity, while Pages in Swords and Wands represent masculine energy of the god, activity, and projection. This inexperienced energy is also idealistic and innocent, regardless of its gendered association.

Whenever you see a Knight, know that the energy is focused on immature energy that aches for knowledge and teachings. Knights in Cups and Pentacles are feminine, while Swords and Wands are masculine, as with Pages. This immature energy of the Knight is also charming and hopeful in its approach, regardless of its gendered association.

Whenever you see a Queen, know that the energy is focused on increased maturity and actualization of goals. As with Pages and Knights, Queens are divided between feminine (Cups and Pentacles) and masculine (Swords and Wands), which affects the energetic interpretation of the card. For example, a Queen of Swords represents actualization of intellectual goals, while the Queen of Wands represents actualization of physical or passionate goals.

Whenever you see a King, know that the energy is focused on responsibility, knowledge, cynicism, and disillusionment. As with the rest of the face cards, there are different gendered associations for Kings based on their suit-type. Ultimately, Kings suggest that what one desired wasn't as fulfilling as one hoped, hence the responsibility *alongside* the disillusionment.

Finally, whenever you see an Ace, know that the energy is focused on new beginnings and hunches for new action. Just like the other suited cards, each suit has a gendered association that affects *where* in one's life he or she will feel or notice these new beginnings. That about sums it up! For your convenience, there is an exercise included in Chapter 5 that will help you to practice this helpful memorization trick!

Trick #5 – Read a Lot!

This memorization trick isn't necessarily the easiest of the bunch, but it will surely be helpful! The gist is to get your hands on as many books about tarot as you can. If you can, get your hands on different types of decks too! Read about the cards' meanings, the imagery, and the way the author talks about memorizing the meanings. Read as much as you can, and the more tarot books you can access, the quicker you'll be able to understand what they mean (and how they all work together).

Chapter 4: The Spreads

Now that you've chosen your deck and have a basic understanding of each card– either in your working memory or to draw upon later in these pages–you are ready for the fun part: doing your own tarot readings! This chapter comes equipped with 20 different spreads so that you can practice with your cards, and each spread has a specific theme or intention. You'll find spreads for introspection and awareness, for each sign in the Western zodiac, for self-diagnosis of illness, and so much more!

Before you do any spread or tarot reading, make sure to cleanse your deck (if it's being used for someone else or if someone else touched your deck recently for any reason), shuffle it well, and put yourself in the moment with all thoughts on what you will ask of the deck.

In order to cleanse your deck, if necessary, the best technique is to use smoke. Light a stick of incense and run your cards through the smoke or apply the same technique with the smoke of burned sage bundles or other dried herbal bundles, incenses, or resins. You can also cleanse your deck with crystals by either making a crystal grid around your deck or by setting a powerful cleansing stone (like Amethyst or Clear Quartz) on top of your deck while you wait. Just about a minute in the smoke or with the crystals should do the trick! Then, shuffle the deck gently while you calm your mind and think of the question you'll be asking.

1. Spread for Past, Present, Future

For this tarot reading, you will focus on where you've come from (your past), where you are now (your present), and where you're about to go (your future). You only need to pull 3 cards, so after you've cleansed and shuffled your deck, think about those three elements: your past, your present, and your future. Think about what you've struggled through and where you hope to be. Lay the three cards face-down first, and arrange them any way you like, but make sure the first represents your past, the second represents your present, and the third represents your future. Flip all three over at once or one at a time to divine your answers.

2. Spread to Identify Three Aspects of the Self

Just like the last spread, you're going to pull only 3 cards, but unlike the last spread, you're going to think about yourself as a whole being rather than about moments in time in your life. After you've cleansed and shuffled the deck, therefore, ask the cards to provide you a glimpse at, for example, your 3 strongest traits, your 3 biggest weaknesses, your 3 biggest lessons for this lifetime, your 3 best job possibilities, or any other 3 major aspects of yourself. As with the first spread, feel free to flip all cards over at once or to interpret one at a time.

3. Spread of Self-Identification (The Grand, or Celtic, Cross)

This spread takes a few more cards to complete than the previous two. You'll need to pull 10 cards for this reading, and you can honestly lay them out any way you like, but the general idea is to make a cross shape with your cards. You can find exact replicas of this spread online if you'd like a picture for assistance, but I'll try to explain it as simply as possible, so you won't have to look elsewhere. Start as usual: cleanse and shuffle your deck. As you're shuffling, choose a question to focus on about yourself or your life.

Lay down your first card in the middle of the space in front of you. Card 1 will represent yourself and your general relationship to the question you're asking. Card 2 will be laid overtop card 1 but sideways, making a cross over that first card, and card 2 will represent any obstacles that directly stand in the way of your path.

Card 3 goes to the left of card 1, and it will represent what is behind you, what you've worked through, and what you can now use to your advantage. Card 4 goes on the other side of card 1, to the right side. It will represent what's generally ahead for you, and what you may need to look out for.

Card 5 goes below card 1, and it suggests something you've grown out of, something that's beneath you that you had to learn from to evolve. Card 6 goes above card 1, and it talks about the best qualities of yourself and the way you access your higher self. Now, by looking at these first 6 cards, you should have that basic cross shape established! Feel free to flip over these cards now and process their meaning in terms of your question.

The next four cards go one after the other in a vertical line next to your cross on its right side. Starting at the bottom, lay card 7, which will represent how you're feeling about moving forward with this new knowledge. Then above card 7, lay card 8, which will demonstrate what the attitudes of people around you are in relation to this matter.

Above card 8 goes card 9, which talks about your greatest fears and hopes in terms of moving forward with this knowledge. Finally, card 10 goes above card 9, and it suggests literally what is to come next, whether that means an experience, a life change, a person, or otherwise. Flip over these four cards now and interpret their meaning alone as well as in reference to the original 6 cards. You'll surely have some questions answered about yourself with this spread!

4. Spread for Aries

This spread will work best for both readers and querents who are Aries (sun sign or ascending/rising sign), so if you're the not an Aries but you're reading the cards for someone who *is*, this might be a great spread to start with! If you *are* an Aries, try this reading out for yourself to see what you can discover!

For this reading, you'll need to pull 7 cards, and you can lay them out any way you like, but make sure you remember the order! Additionally, you don't necessarily have to ask a question in association with this spread, for you can simply learn from the cards as they fall. But if a question lays heavy on your heart as an Aries, it will certainly find some resolution through this reading, too.

Card 1 will represent how you're doing physically. Card 2 will demonstrate how your overall energy level is, and card 3 asks how you're doing in terms of control. Are you uncontrolled? Or are you reigned in and focused on succeeding? Card 3 will have something to say about that.

Card 4 talks about how your excitement is for life, and how enthusiastic you're feeling. Card 5 asks what you're running away from in life, Aries. Card 6 shows you how to best approach your goals and dreams, and card 7 reveals what those deepest, truest goals and dreams really are. Lay down your cards one at a time and process them individually for the best results.

5. Spread for Taurus

Similarly, for the Aries spread, this one works best for Taurus readers and querents, so be aware! This Taurus reading requires 7 cards, and they can also be laid out any way the reader wants. Again, you don't really need to ask a question with this spread, for it will provide good advice and direction for Taurus regardless.

Card 1 asks Taurus to dig deep and investigate what his or her opinions and stances on money and possessions are right now. Card 2 looks at the state of your current finances, and card 3 peers a little deeper by examining what skills and talents you're using to make this income.

Card 4 wonders whether Taurus has been feeling sexual pleasure recently (and if so, how the experiences were). Card 5 looks at how Taurus relates to luxury and excess, while card 6 questions how patient Taurus has been able to be lately. Finally, card 7 examines jealousy and possessiveness outside material goods. Ideally, this card will show where Taurus's biggest struggles currently lie. As with the Aries spread, lay down each card one at a time, and process each one before moving forward.

6. Spread for Gemini

Along the same lines as the previous two spreads, this one will work best for readers and querents who are Gemini (sun sign or ascending), and you will have to pull 8 cards for this reading. As with the other astrological readings, you can lay out your cards any way you like, and it's best to lay them out one at a time and process them individually. (Again, you don't really need to ask a question with this spread, for it will provide good advice and direction for Gemini regardless.)

Card 1 for Gemini's spread talks about how your mind is working right now. Card 2 checks on your truth and wonders how well you can lie at the moment, and card 3 wonders what (or who) you might be researching or watching presently.

Card 4 talks about family and checks in with how things are going for you with your parents and siblings. Card 5 looks at communication: how are things going? Do you fight more than you agree? Do you communicate pleasantly or aggressively? What happens when you *do* get into a fight? Consider these questions for card 5.

Card 6 discusses doubt for Gemini. What's holding you back with the power of doubt? Card 7 wonders if you're being delusional or too dreamy about anything in your life, and card 8 is the kicker for Gemini, the sign of the twins: how is your relationship with your inner twin, and what is your inner twin like?

7. Spread for Cancer

For any Cancers out there, it's time for your spread, and you'll want to pull 8 cards for this reading. Again you can arrange them any way you like but be sure to process them one at a time. (You don't really need to ask a question with this spread, for it will provide good advice and direction for Cancer regardless.)

Card 1 tells Cancer where he or she comes from, as in what family circumstances birthed this person and what complexities may have helped shape him or her. Card 2 asks you what your dreams are, Cancer! Card 3 wonders how your current home life is, and card 4 specifically questions how you view your father.

Card 5 shows you how much you *need* a security net to feel happy and safe in the world, and card 6 asks you how (or how intensely) you express your deepest feelings. Card 7 talks about your compassion: how kind and considerate are you, really? And finally, card 8 questions how psychic you are (or will be) and how awakened and advanced your abilities are right now.

8. Spread for Leo

This spread for Leos works like the other astrological readings in that it's best for Leo readers and querents. You'll pull 7 cards for this spread, and you can arrange them any way you like, but be sure to process them one at a time. (Again, you don't really need to ask a question with this spread, for it will provide good advice and direction for Leo regardless.)

Card 1 questions how intense and dominating your ego is right now, Leo. Card 2 sees the world as a stage and wonders what part of that stage you're acting on these days. Card 3 looks within you for your inner child, to see if he or she is there and how healthy that "child" is today. Card 4 wonders about your love life: how are things going and how are you feeling about love and romance right now?

Card 5 examines your admiration, respect, and compassion for children, and card 6 looks at where you take risks and relish in risky freedoms. Finally, card 7 looks to your Leonine mane. While you may be king or queen of the jungle, are you a generous ruler or a wicked one?

9. Spread for Virgo

This spread for Virgos works like the other astrological readings in that it's best for Virgo readers and querents. You'll pull 8 cards for this spread, and you can arrange them any way you like, but be sure to process them one at a time. (Again, you don't really need to ask a question with this spread, for it will provide good advice and direction for Virgo regardless).

When you pull card 1 for Virgo, it will reveal pieces of how you feel about your body as an aspect of yourself. Card 2 will reveal how interested you are in healing or medical studies. Card 3 talks about your physical health at this moment, and card 4 questions how you're feeling about work.

Card 5 wonders how your analytical mind is working and whether you're being too critical. Card 6 looks at how easily you adjust after hardship, and card 7 reveals how consistent you are and whether you're a hypocrite. This card will show you if you're being too much of a perfectionist, too. Finally, card 8 wonders how distanced you are from life because of being too wary.

10. Spread for Libra

This spread for Libras works like the other astrological readings in that it's best for Libra readers and querents. You'll pull 9 cards for this spread, and you can arrange them any way you like, but be sure to process them one at a time. (Again, you don't really need to ask a question with this spread, for it will provide good advice and direction for Libra regardless.)

Libra's first card will talk about decision making, since Libras stereotypically have a hard time making decisions. Card 2 shows how you form relationships with others and how you socially bond. Card 3 looks at how you bond with others in a professional or vocational setting, and card 4 is more about where in your life you (strive to) fight for peace.

Card 5 reveals your potential for forgiveness or vengeance and which of the two is more familiar to you. Card 6 looks at your intimate relationships and wonders what you give away of yourself to these lovers. Card 7 encourages you to see how you might be repressing or suppressing some of your feelings, and card 8 interprets how artistic your feelings can be. Finally, card 9 looks to your worst traits: how do you act (or appear) phony and sullen?

11. Spread for Scorpio

This spread for Scorpios works like the other astrological readings in that it's best for Scorpio readers and querents. You'll pull 8 cards for this spread, and you can arrange them any way you like, but be sure to process them one at a time. (Again, you don't really need to ask a question with this spread, for it will provide good advice and direction for Scorpio regardless.)

The first card for Scorpios relates to card 7 from the Libra spread: what are you emotionally suppressing, and what tends to get suppressed more than anything else? Card 2 forces you to face your taboos, and card 3 encourages you to embrace your true sexuality. Card 4 shows you how you conceptualize your own death, and card 5 reveals your innermost values (in case you didn't already name them).

Card 6 shows what potential legacies and birthrights will be yours, and card 7 gets personal by forcing you to face your own tendency (or tendencies) for self-destruction. Finally, card 8 likens you to water, like the element of Scorpio itself: are you a creek, a lake, a river, or an ocean? In other words, how deep are you and what is your capacity for (spiritual, emotional, and intellectual) intensity in this life?

12. Spread for Sagittarius

This spread for Sagittarius works like the other astrological readings in that it's best for Sagittarius readers and querents. You'll pull 6 cards for this spread, and you can arrange them any way you like, but be sure to process them one at a time. (Again, you don't really need to ask a question with this spread, for it will provide good advice and direction for Sagittarius regardless.)

The first card for Sagittarius represents how you're interacting with your social sphere. What role do you play in these environments? Card 2 examines how your education has been up until now, and card 3 looks to your most firmly-held beliefs or practices of religion. Card 4 reveals the extent (or impact) of journeying and adventuring you've done in the outside world, while card 5 does the same for any journeying and travelling you may have done (or that you may be doing now) in reference to your own inner world. Finally, card 6 shows where you are on your life-long search for meaning and purpose (as well as what you can expect from the near future!).

13. Spread for Capricorn

This spread for Capricorns works like the other astrological readings in that it's best for Capricorn readers and querents. You'll pull 7 cards for this spread, and you can arrange them any way you like, but be sure to process them one at a time. (Again, you don't really need to ask a question with this spread, for it will provide good advice and direction for Capricorn regardless.)

Card 1 for Capricorns looks at how you feel about your career and what hopes you sense for that vocational future. Card 2 reveals how intense your wishes for power and fame are, while card 3 looks at how you are as an individual: are you as intense as your wishes for power, are you serious, and are you responsible?

Card 4 shows how your values line up with the values of the world as a whole, and card 5 examines your relationship with your mother in this lifetime. Card 6 highlights what you should aim for, as far as your goals and successes in this world. Finally, card 7 reveals what you're aiming toward with all this hard work, thoughtfulness, and dedication.

14. Spread for Aquarius

This spread for Aquarius works like the other astrological readings in that it's best for Aquarius readers and querents. You'll pull 8 cards for this spread, and you can arrange them any way you like, but be sure to process them one at a time. (Again, you don't really need to ask a question with this spread, for it will provide good advice and direction for Aquarius regardless.)

For Aquarius, your first card will demonstrate the closest friends in your life right now and what they represent for you. Card 2 shows you how you're feeling about freedom and whether you're trapped in any aspect of your life right now. Card 3 points to your role in the group: are you a leader, a worker, a follower, or what? Card 4 is all about opposition: what do you work against in the current society you inhabit? What revolutionary urges do you hold deeply?

Card 5 reveals how impulsive you can be, and card 6 looks at whether you're feeling worthy, superior, or inferior to others in this lifetime. Card 7 asks whether you're underestimating yourself or if you've got an inflated sense of self instead, and finally, card 8 shows you the path you must follow to be able to live out your dreams and follow your stars.

15. Spread for Pisces

This spread for Pisces works like the other astrological readings in that it's best for Pisces readers and querents. You'll pull 7 cards for this spread, and you can arrange them any way you like, but be sure to process them one at a time. (Again, you don't really need to ask a question with this spread, for it will provide good advice and direction for Pisces regardless.)

Pisces' first card wonders how idealistic and optimistic you are, or–the converse–how pessimistic or realistic you tend to be instead. Card 2 cuts to the core and reveals your tendency for self-sacrifice or martyrdom (either intellectually or emotionally). Card 3 shows the spiritual path you've been on and where it may lead you.

Pisces is the escapist of the Western zodiac, and the reading will keep things real by demonstrating what you're addicted to in this life with card 4. Card 5 reveals any hidden adversaries that may be creeping into your life, while card 6 points out where you may be metaphorically imprisoned or stuck. Finally, card 7 draws out the path that will save you from these setbacks and what you have to look forward to once you're liberated.

16. Spread for Self-Diagnosis of Dis-ease

For this tarot reading, we'll move away from astrological themes and towards health. This spread intends to explain, decipher, and locate the source of your internal or external dis-ease. You'll pull 5 cards for this spread, and it's ideal that you sit on the ground to do this reading because you'll arrange those 5 cards around you like five points of a star with you at the center.

Card 1 will be placed directly in front of you, and it signifies the source of your power, how you gain energy, and how your body then uses that energy. Card 2 will be placed to your right as the second point on the star, and it represents what you're currently feeling inside, in terms of dis-ease. Card 3 will be placed to your right and slightly behind you as the third point on the star. It suggests where that dis-ease might spiritually or emotionally come from.

Card 4 will be placed to your left and slightly behind you, and it represents what influences of others or what past life struggles may be making this dis-ease more pronounced for you right now. Finally, card 5 will be placed to your left as the final point of the star. This card signifies how you can turn things around and how you can begin to approach self-directed healing for this dis-ease.

17. Spread for the New Year

This simple 12-card spread can be used for any culture's New Year celebration, as long as the culture in question still relies on a 12-month calendar! You'll pull 1 card for each month, and you can lay them all face down before turning them over one at a time to process. While you shuffle the deck after cleansing, you can either let the cards generally predict major themes of the year ahead, or you can always infuse your reading with a particular theme or question that you'd like answered.

18. Spread for Your Birthday!

For your birthday this year, do a tarot spread for what's coming! It's absolutely simple, and you can pull any number of cards that you'd like. My go-to birthday reading is to do a 3-card pull, with the first card representing the past year that I leave behind, the second card signifying what I bring to the next year, and the third card suggesting how the next year will allow me to grow. You could also do a 12-card spread for each month of the upcoming year (like the previous New Year spread), a 4- or 5-card spread for each week in your birthday month, a 7-card spread for each day of your birthday week, or a 1-card pull for the biggest lesson you'll have to face this year.

19. Spread of the Pyramid (Facets of the Self)

This 6-card spread demonstrates 6 different sides of the self, and each card will be laid out to form the overall shape of a pyramid. Ancient Egyptians believed that there were numerous facets of the self, some of which we freely share with others and some of which we keep hidden. Therefore, there will be some sides of the self that become revealed in this tarot reading that you'll struggle to face, but once you do, you'll be able to grow in ways you may have never considered for yourself.

When you pull card 1, imagine that you're starting to build the base of your pyramid. You can leave it on its back and wait until you "build" your entire card pyramid, or you can turn it over immediately to see the side of the self that you're proud of, what you've grown consciously and are eager to share with others. Card 2 will go to the right of card 1, and it will represent the side of the self you're ashamed of and what you keep hidden at all costs. Card 3 goes to the right of card 2 and suggests the side of you that will sacrifice anything for others, the martyr side.

Card 4 will establish the second row of the pyramid, so put it above cards 1 and 2, yet right in between them. This card demonstrates the side of yourself that's a scholar, a lover of knowledge. For what area of study do you feel this love, and what do you do when you feel it? Card 5 goes to the right of card 4, and it should be above and between cards 2 and 3. This card signifies the side of the self that is a lover. How do you love, who do you love, and how can you share that with the world? Finally, card 6 will make the top of the pyramid in a row above cards 4 and 5 but right between them. This card represents the final aspect of your pyramid, which is how you bring all these other facets together and fuse them into your identity and self-expression.

20. Spread for the Week Ahead

Similar to the New Year spread, which requires a card for each month in the year, this reading for the week ahead requires as many cards as there are days in the week. Once you've pulled those 7 cards, arrange them any way you like, and overturn them individually or all at once. Whether you start your mental calendar on Monday or Sunday, the first card you lay down may vary, so go by what feels right to you. For me, card 1 is Sunday, card 2 is Monday, card 3 is Tuesday, etc. This reading will give you a great sense of what to expect from the week ahead whenever you need a psychic boost!

While some of these tarot spreads are more complicated or involved than others, they all demonstrate a very good place to start. They're accessible, they're easy to understand, they're insightful, and they're going to be extremely helpful in both your life as a whole and your growing relationship with the tarot. You can find any number of additional spreads in other books and online, but you can also invent your own tarot readings as you go! Try these for a start, then unleash the floodgates! There's so much to be explored.

Chapter 5: Exercises & Brain Boosters

If you're still looking for more to do with the tarot aside from simply looking at the cards to learn them or trying readings out on yourself, fear not! You haven't reached the end of the road with tarot, for there's so much more you can do. This chapter provides 10 exercises with the cards that you can play around with in order to better understand what tarot is all about.

There is a difficulty rating included in the explanation of each exercise so that you will know what you're getting yourself into. The rating uses a simple scale of 1 to 3, with 1 being super easy, 2 being average difficulty, and 3 being more complicated. Additionally, before this chapter ends, you'll receive 3 tips to use as brain boosters with your overall tarot experience. There's a lot to learn, so dive right in!

Exercise #1 – Find Your Tarot Card for the Year

This exercise will take you deeper into the meaning of one card each year, and the card linked with you will become incredibly symbolic for your next 12 months. On the turn of the New Year, as the year number ticks up to one more, you can figure out your tarot Growth Card for the year ahead. All you have to do is add the day and month of your birthday with the digits of the new year. For example, say your birthday is 5/25/1961, and it just became 2019. You'd add 5 (the month) + 2 + 5 (the day) to get 12 and then add 12 + 2 + 0 + 1 + 9 to get your ending number of 24.

Then, you'd associate this number with its corresponding card in the Major Arcana. However, there are only 22 cards in the Major Arcana, so if you get to a number greater than 22 (like this example's 24), you'd add the individual digits of the number to find which card links with you instead. For example, 24 becomes 2 + 4, which is 6, so the corresponding Major Arcana card for this person in this New Year would be the Lovers. By looking at this card closely for its symbolism and by analyzing all its potential meanings, this person will discover what the upcoming year has in store for him or her.

Difficulty level: 1

Exercise #2 – Gather a Few Decks Together

This exercise is designed to help you understand the symbolism behind the cards rather than just the information, meanings, and words packed within them. I can explain what each card means until the cows come home, but sometimes that just doesn't stick. Instead, you can get visual with your deck! And if you have multiple decks, combine them and see what the different artists were thinking about, say, the Moon card or the Strength card.

This type of close looking is a great way to perceive the messages behind the images, for there are so many images and symbols within the pictures of each card that can allow you to understand their meanings better than any book of descriptions could. Essentially, if you can, gather together a few decks and look to the imagery in the pictures. Take notes if you want, but even just by looking, you will expand your appreciation of the cards greatly.

Difficulty level: 2 (simply due to the cost of acquiring several decks)

Exercise #3 – Pull a Daily Card

To become more familiar with your deck in particular (as well as the cards in general), you are absolutely invited to start pulling a daily card! This practice is extremely effective to help newcomers to tarot become more understanding of what their decks (and the tarot overall) can offer. It's up to you whether you pull your card in the morning, in mid-day, or the evening after everything's already happened, but the point is to draw a card each day so that you're constantly practicing with the deck while boosting your divination and psychic abilities.

For those who are actually newcomers to tarot, I always recommend starting this exercise with all the cards facing the same direction. Without the "reversed" card option in play, you can get a solid working knowledge of what the cards mean generally. Then, after a few weeks or months of pulling a card a day, when you're ready to add in the "reversed" option, please do! You'll find that waiting to add in this layer of tarot can really help for those who are either overwhelmed or confused.

Difficulty level: 1

Exercise #4 – Download a Tarot App

If you don't have your own deck yet (or if you don't want to bring your deck everywhere with you), try downloading an app for tarot on your phone or tablet! There are so many good tarot apps out there, and many of them are free. Frequently, apps of this type offer options for daily readings, bigger tarot spreads, individual card information, and sometimes even journaling based on what cards you pull.

It may seem ingenuine to approach the tarot technologically, but the same rules apply as will be explained in tip #3 later on. You're in charge, not the cards and not the app. Your higher self is who and what guides the reading and who delivers the overall meaning. So, don't knock the app option until you've tried it! You may be surprised how much it helps to have a virtual deck with you on the go everywhere. When it comes down to it, it's also just a helpful, handy, informative option! The quicker you get familiar with these cards, the better!

Difficulty level: 1

Exercise #5 – Make a Chart for Your Daily Pulls

For those who are extra studious and who love making lists, you're bound to attach to exercise 5 immediately. The goal of this exercise is to allow you to track the cards you've pulled in the past year, to note patterns, and to observe themes in your readings based on what's happened in your life. All you have to do is start a daily practice of pulling one card each day. Then, it's time to get crafty.

You'll want to make a big chart with maybe 10 columns going across the top, and every card of the tarot deck making rows going down the side. Based on the card you pull each day, you'll mark it on the chart which one it was, and then after a month, a few months, or a year, you will see how frequently you've pulled each card as well as which ones you may have somehow avoided. Based on these frequencies and accidental avoidances, you'll find which themes have played out in the past month, months, or year, and you can enhance your overall understanding of the cards, too.

Difficulty level: 3 (requires focus & consistency over time as well as creativity)

Exercise #6 – What Does the Card Want You to Know?

This exercise is kind of like doing a tarot reading in reverse. Often, you know what you will be laying out, how many cards there will be, and what each card will symbolize. However, this exercise turns that method on its head and thereby helps you access your connection to your higher self (and to the cards) better. Ultimately, you'll still cleanse, shuffle, and vibe with the deck as usual. You can still ask the deck an overall question or feel a certain energy when you shuffle, hoping for answers and resolutions. The trick is that you won't know what you're pulling for until you pull the card.

You'll want to be very open, centered, and grounded when you attempt this exercise because it is a little more difficult. You also want to be so open and grounded because you're going to have to dig deeper with yourself and the cards this time after asking your question. When you pull each card, sit with it for a few moments before flipping it over so that you can let your higher self tell you which aspect of your question this card refers to.

You can pull as many cards as needed, and I recommend trying to take note of what they signify as soon as you pick up on that information from your higher self. That way, when you finally flip the cards over, you'll still remember what each one relates to in reference to your overall question. At that point, you can conduct your reading, as usual, to see how your question has been answered.

Difficulty level: 3 (requires hefty intuition & psychic focus)

Exercise #7 – Find a Tarot "Study Buddy"

It might not seem imminently helpful, but another person getting interested in tarot with you can mean all the difference for some beginning practitioners! Group work can be incredibly beneficial in reference to tarot because the people in the group become accountable to one another, and fierce study of the cards can be instigated. Furthermore, working with at least one other person can keep the information fresh, enabling you to understand more about the tarot even faster. I hope that you will end up doing readings for one another to put the knowledge into practice!

Difficulty level: 2

Exercise #8 – Associate Your Own Keywords for Each Card

This exercise is for those more studious individuals who want to understand their cards' meanings quickly with no dilly-dallying! The gist of the exercise is to go through all the cards in the deck, and in a journal or notebook somewhere, take note of 2-4 keywords that describe each one. Eventually, you may be able to use your notebook of keywords when you're conducting your readings more than you use the information provided in this book! Regardless of how you use it, putting this massive store of information into your own words and then writing all that down allows your brain to process every piece of knowledge better and more holistically.

For those who are increasingly studious and looking for even more work, I recommend doing the same exercise for the "reversed" meanings of the cards as well. On the other hand, you could always write 2 keywords for the standard card placement and 2 more keywords for the "reversed" placement right away in the same journal! However, you choose to do it, this exercise will absolutely help you understand your deck better, and it will give you a powerful psychic and confidence boost for all your future readings.

Difficulty level: 2 (requires a fair amount of effort)

Exercise #9 – Try it with Court Cards Only

Sometimes, people are just overwhelmed with the entire tarot deck, so I'll recommend an exercise based on slimming things down. Essentially, you can take out any segment of the tarot deck and use that for your reading instead of the entire deck. I like to choose related segments of the deck for exercises of this type. For example, this exercise in particular recommends you try a few readings using only the court (or face) cards in the Minor Arcana.

There are 56 cards in the Minor Arcana compared to the 22 of the Major Arcana, so even just working with the entire Minor segment can be a lot for an overwhelmed practitioner. Slim things down even further by pulling out all the Aces, Pages, Knights, Queens, and Kings of each set and using just them for a few readings. Readings of this nature are best suited for questions regarding bigger life events or queries about people in your life. You're sure to get some firm answers to your questions, but you'll also learn so much more about these 20 cards in the tarot deck than you would if they were just 20 out of 56 (or 20 out of 78).

Difficulty level: 1

Exercise #10 – Try it with Major Arcana Only

Similar to exercise 9, this exercise focuses on reading one's fortune using only the 22 Major Arcana cards. These cards demonstrate the major events in one's lifetime, so questions best suited for this type of reading are ones relating to the "flavor" of one's life direction, what stage of life you're inhabiting, and what your overall goals in this lifetime should be.

Difficulty level: 1

Now to break things up in terms of these exercises, it's time to get straight to the tips! If you're feeling overwhelmed by the tarot, confused, unsure, or misdirected, touch back in with these tips, and you won't go wrong, I promise. Additionally, if you need just a little support or positive and encouraging advice, come back to these tips, too. They're sure to remind you of how powerful you (and your tarot deck) can be.

Tip #1 – Don't Overreach or Overwhelm Yourself!

If you do happen to feel overwhelmed in consideration of the tarot, try not to panic, and don't let yourself give up! These cards demonstrate powerful energetic archetypes that can teach us so much, and it would be a shame for you to give up simply because there's a lot of information! Of course, there is! Remind yourself to see the fun in that knowledge, and when you are feeling overwhelmed, try to scale things back to a more simple approach. Try a simpler reading or use exercises 9 or 10 to scale the deck back to a manageable amount of information. Process a little at a time, and you will be able to release this feeling in no time.

For those that aren't necessarily overwhelmed by the tarot but who are, perhaps, trying to do too much, consider this: you may be doing a lot *with* the cards, but do you really *know* them yet? Do you actually remember any of the spreads you've done, and are you starting to remember any particular cards? The goal is to answer these questions with a firm and resounding "yes," so if you need to re-simplify and rescale things to a more manageable amount of content (even if you feel like you don't need this step), don't be ashamed! Go ahead with the rescaling and then you'll re-emerge with confidence, knowledge, and true *ability* to handle all this overreaching from before.

Tip #2 – Keep a Tarot Journal

Anyone who reads tarot cards will benefit from keeping a tarot journal. You don't even need a physical notebook, for you can keep notes on your phone these days! Note what cards appear often, and what cards you're particularly drawn to. Note how you're feeling about your readings, how accurate they are, and how you intend to proceed with your life afterward. The more you're processing this bulk of information, the better you'll be able to integrate the learning experiences into your life, so don't be afraid to jot down things that feel important!

However works for you, start recording those tarot experiences, tarot readings, and intense card pulls. With time, you may notice patterns between the cards pulled and events in your life or emotional moments. You may also notice your psychic powers and intuition growing, and those things are equally important to take note of! Embrace the change tarot offers by keeping a record of every life-altering realization. In a few years, you'll be a tarot expert with this practice.

Tip #3 – Remember Who's in Charge!

I know it's still likely hard to imagine, but when you're doing tarot readings, you're the star. Your higher self connects with you through the archetypes in the cards, and that connection enables you to answer these questions truthfully and provide direction for your future. When you're feeling overwhelmed or frustrated by the tarot, don't let your anger with the cards get in the way! It's not their fault! You're still learning, and that's absolutely okay. Allow yourself to be patient, to be forgiven, and to be the one in charge of the experience.

If you're frustrated because you don't understand the messages the cards are telling you, try to remember that it might be *you* who's not open to receiving the messages. It's not the cards being worthless or bad quality; it's probably not even that they're wrong. When you feel this frustration, just remember that the power of tarot lies within your own soul. Open yourself to the message, and try approaching the spread again. Don't get upset with yourself, either, when things get frustrating or confusing! It's all a practice that will settle and solidify within you in time. Learning may be tough, but your future self will be so grateful you took the time.

Chapter 6: Extensions of Tarot

Tarot has intimate and innate connections with the worlds of numerology and astrology. Each card is associated with a number, and each number has a specific meaning that can help you understand the cards better. Furthermore, each card has an archetypal energy that links well with the symbols of the Western zodiac. Tarot looks at these astrological symbols and elemental energies and sees the reflection of some of its own cards and energies.

This chapter will be dedicated to hashing out these intimate and innate connections. We will first walk through the power of numerology in relation to tarot before engaging in astrological and elemental associations. I hope that by the end of this chapter, you will have a few more tricks to memorize your deck, and you will also be able to understand the power of the symbols that run through all of these powerful divination systems (including tarot reading, numerology, astrology, among so many others). You'll be an expert in reading the tarot in no time with these important informational extensions in place.

Tarot & Numerology

The 3rd memorization trick in Chapter 3 hinted that numbers have a deep meaning that often goes unacknowledged. Tarot is a great realm to finally acknowledge that truth. Furthermore, that 3rd trick suggested that by memorizing the numerological associations, remembering major themes in your deck becomes easy and so much more accessible. The details of those associations will be revealed below.

Remember that every card is associated with a number, and most decks will print the number directly on the card for your ease. The Major Arcana number from 1-22 (or 0), and the Minor Arcana go from Aces to Kings, which technically number from 0 to 14. Look to the number on the card and align it with the card's element (recall that trick #2 in Chapter 3 reveals these associations) to have a basic understanding of the entire deck without needing a book in your hands at all.

The Meaning of 0 (Zero)

Zero is said to represent all that exists as potential in the universe. 0 is the connection we share with everything else through the simple fact that we exist. We are here now, and that means we can be anything. 0 reveals that potential. 0 also demonstrates the concepts of connectedness, understanding, and wholeness.

The Meaning of 1

The Number 1 is said to represent new beginnings, taking initiatives, and finding a simple sense of completion. It is a number fulfilled in itself, and it has its own internal balance that doesn't depend on anything else. 1 demonstrates the promise of something good coming, and it also relates to one's powers of manifestation.

The Meaning of 2

The Number 2 is said to represent one's relationships with others. It signifies connectivity, intimacy, and romance as well as platonic relationships of all sorts. 2 is about interplay, interactivity, and the choice you have within all those varying options. 2 demonstrates all that experience with others has to teach you.

The Meaning of 3

The Number 3 is said to represent what happens as a product of union. 2 is about that union in many senses, but 3 reveals the creative product, result, or outcome. 3 is the essence of creativity and expression. Furthermore, it demonstrates the path of growth. 3 demonstrates the importance and value of synthesis.

The Meaning of 4

The Number 4 is said to represent stability, home life, and structure. 4 is all about what happens under 4 walls, or what becomes complete with a 4th line: the square. The square additionally symbolizes numerological perfection in some ways. 4 is a number that exists within nature too as a backbone and stabilizer, so it demonstrates this material world we inhabit.

The Meaning of 5

The Number 5 is said to represent both health and crisis in health. It is the same number as there are points on a star, which relates to the pentagram (associated with selflessness and goodness) and the pentacle (its inverse, associated with self-focus and variability). 5 is a divine number that reveals a transformation will come; however, it also demonstrates the extremes of that transformation potential.

The Meaning of 6

The Number 6 is said to represent natural harmony or balance, and it is another number that suggests a union is in order. In this case, 6 represents the divine marriage between divine masculine and divine feminine, which can take place within each individual as well as between individuals in the world. It's a number that demonstrates connection and the integrated knowledge that will emerge from it.

The Meaning of 7

The Number 7 is said to represent magic itself. 7 is the number of mysteries, the occult, the divine, and what remains hidden (although often in plain sight). This number correlates with expanded education on many levels, too, whether that occurs through self-guided study, spiritual practice, metaphorically going back to basics, or literally going back to school. In sum, 7 demonstrates what can happen when you experiment, take risks, research, and develop your own inner magic.

The Meaning of 8

The Number 8 is said to represent abundance itself. 8 is also a manifestation number that's intimately connected with the divine. In many pagan calendars, 8 holy holidays were celebrated, and 8 still represents the number of seasonal holidays we hold dear. 8 demonstrates the importance of worship and celebration, as well as all that comes from that: prosperity and the essence of abundance.

The Meaning of 9

The Number 9 is said to represent completion that aims toward leadership. You are following a cycle that's about to be completed, and that will mean new options for you. 9 signifies this energy. Furthermore, 9 demonstrates what happens when you're fully selfless and allow yourself to be directed by divinity. 9 is about the healing that can be enacted for self and others when you're openly loving.

The Meaning of 10

The Number 10 combines the energies of 1 and 0; it is said to represent new beginnings like the number 1, but it's more importantly about how endings are often new beginnings in disguise, using that essential energy of 0, too. 10 is a number of culmination and things ending. It is also a number that demonstrates freshness and transformation.

The Meaning of 11

The Number 11 combines the energies of 1 and 1; it is said to represent spiritual awakening. In the tarot, 11 associates with Pages from the Minor Arcana and with the Justice card from the Major Arcana, but the number itself represents intuition, inspiration, and connection with one's higher self. 11 demonstrates the importance of listening both to one's inner voice and to the voices of the world in order to establish ethics, morality, direction, and a sense of righteousness.

The Meaning of 12

The Number 12 combines the energies of 1 and 2; it is said to represent new beginnings based on liberation, independence, and self-reliance. In the tarot, 12 associates with Knights from the Minor Arcana and with the Hanged Man card from the Major Arcana, but the number itself represents what happens when you realize your life purpose and/or soul mission: everything fake fades away, and you become the most authentic version of yourself possible. 12 demonstrates that capability.

The Meaning of 13

The Number 13 combines the energies of 1 and 3; it is said to represent one's powers of manifestation. In the tarot, 13 associates with Queens from the Minor Arcana and with the Death card from the Major Arcana, but the number itself represents that what seems harsh may be exactly what you asked for. 13 shows you how your circumstances are more of your making than you may have realized before, yet it also demonstrates potential to break new ground with this realization.

The Meaning of 14

The Number 14 combines the energies of 1 and 4; it is said to represent a warning regarding money matters and that some test may be coming soon. In the tarot, 14 associates with Kings from the Minor Arcana and with Temperance from the Major Arcana, but the number itself represents sacrifices you may have to make if you desire to achieve your goals. It demonstrates beneficial challenges ahead that will result in lasting successes.

The Meaning of 15

The Number 15 combines the energies of 1 and 5; it is said to represent your increasing awareness that positive change is coming. You're about to realize what's been holding you back all along, and that may be painful, but you'll emerge stronger than ever. 15 reminds you to keep your eyes on the prize so that you aren't held back by the struggles that lay ahead. It demonstrates resilience, strength, needed transformation, and introspection.

The Meaning of 16

The Number 16 combines the energies of 1 and 6; it is said to represent material success to come. 16 is all about your ability to turn obstacles into positive outcomes, and the number suggests that you may find the next example of this ability sooner than you thought. 16 encourages you to have faith and stand strong, for it demonstrates how your willpower will win out after all.

The Meaning of 17

The Number 17 combines the energies of 1 and 7; it is said to represent an aspect of levelling up in your life. For the most part, 17 relates to levelled-up manifestation experience. Your intuition will be your greatest guide through this adaptation, but remember that big changes are imminent! 17 demonstrates how you'll have to step up to the plate for this levelling up to occur.

The Meaning of 18

The Number 18 combines the energies of 1 and 8; it is said to represent increased discernment, wisdom, and confidence. The outcome of such positivity will be increased capacity for abundance, which works well after 17 gave you all the manifestation experience you could need. 18 will encourage you to use all that abundance for the benefit of mankind, too. 18 is selfless, if not somewhat idealistic, and that is a beautiful combination.

The Meaning of 19

The Number 19 combines the energies of 1 and 9; it is said to represent something similar to what number 10 does--showing us that endings often provide the best and freshest new beginnings. 19 is the number that reveals your divine purpose and connects you with that experience. It's about the inherent stability that can be provided by self-help, and it demonstrates the changes you can incorporate into your life when you are able to face your darkest sides.

The Meaning of 20

The Number 20 combines the energies of 2 and 0; it is said to represent that harmony is coming your way as long as you live with compassion, love, and connection to your intuition. 20 also encourages action with others that validates these gifts of compassion, love, and intuition. Through appropriate action, harmony can be established, and 20 demonstrates that beautiful and liberating potential.

The Meaning of 21

The Number 21 combines the energies of 2 and 1; it is said to represent pure energy in expression, whether verbally, physically, or metaphysically. 21 is a manifestation number as well as a transformative one, and it encourages taking new directions with your new modes of expression. 21 accompanies charisma and genuine communication with others, demonstrating a more evolved version of the self.

The Meaning of 22

The Number 22 combines the energies of 2 and 2; it is said to represent accomplishment and acquired power. 22 is also a number representative of successful partnerships, but this could have pertinence for one's vocational endeavors more so than romantic ones. 22 demonstrates how confidence and hard work pay off and how blessings abound when a harmonious life is achieved.

Tarot & Western Astrology (and more)

Every sign of the zodiac in Western astrology relates with an archetypal energy from the tarot deck. This section will show you how to recognize those relations, since they are admittedly less than obvious. It's not so simple to say that Aries links with the Magician because they're both #1 in their respective areas of study. It's not so simple at all but worry not! I'll guide you through the associations, and it will be accessible enough in no time.

Tarot Looks at Aries...

...and sees the Emperor card from the Major Arcana. Both have energies of determination, commitment, applied authority, motivation, loyalty, and reliability. If you're an Aries conducting a reading for yourself (or if you're reading for someone else who's an Aries), choose the Emperor card to represent yourself (or the Aries querent in question) if the reading asks for a card of this type. Additionally, if the Emperor card arises in an Aries person's spread, it likely represents that person him or herself.

Tarot Looks at Taurus...

...and sees the Hierophant card from the Major Arcana. Both are intense and piercing, they cannot be superficial, and they're deeply involved in truth as a tradition. If you're a Taurus conducting a reading for yourself (or if you're reading for someone else who's a Taurus), choose the Hierophant card to represent yourself (or the Taurus querent in question) if the reading asks for a card of this type. Additionally, if the Hierophant card arises in a Taurus person's spread, it likely represents that person him or herself.

Tarot Looks at Gemini...

...and sees the Lovers card from the Major Arcana. Both are involved with turning points, weighty decisions, careful proceedings, and maintaining personal integrity. If you're a Gemini conducting a reading for yourself (or if you're reading for someone else who's a Gemini), choose the Lovers card to represent yourself (or the Gemini querent in question) if the reading asks for a card of this type. Additionally, if the Lovers card arises in a Gemini person's spread, it likely represents that person him or herself.

Tarot Looks at Cancer...

...and sees the Chariot card from the Major Arcana. Both are transcendent, steady, security-seeking, partially-protected or - shielded freedom-loving, intuitive, and road-opening. If you're a Cancer conducting a reading for yourself (or if you're reading for someone else who's a Cancer), choose the Chariot card to represent yourself (or the Cancer querent in question) if the reading asks for a card of this type. Additionally, if the Chariot card arises in a Cancer person's spread, it likely represents that person him or herself.

Tarot Looks at Leo...

...and sees the Strength card from the Major Arcana. Both are strong, emotional, mental, courageous, and physical. They both prefer to face their problems with grace rather than avoid them entirely. If you're a Leo conducting a reading for yourself (or if you're reading for someone who's a Leo), choose the Strength card to represent yourself (or the Leo querent in question) if the reading asks for a card of this type. Additionally, if the Strength card arises in a Leo person's spread, it likely represents that person him or herself.

Tarot Looks at Virgo...

...and sees the Hermit card from the Major Arcana. Both are purposeful yet slow, wary yet innocent, experienced and wise yet young at heart, exploratory but only on the inside, and open to the world yet guarded. If you're a Virgo conducting a reading for yourself (or if you're reading for someone who's a Virgo), choose the Hermit card to represent yourself (or the Virgo querent in question) if the reading asks for a card of this type. Additionally, if the Hermit card arises in a Virgo person's spread, it likely represents that person him or herself.

Tarot Looks at Libra...

...and sees the Justice card from the Major Arcana. Both are desirous, emotional, light-hearted, righteous, fair, and justice-oriented. Both also should be careful to note the difference between what is desire versus what is need. If you're a Libra conducting a reading for yourself (or if you're reading for someone else who's a Libra), choose the Justice card to represent yourself (or the Libra querent in question) if the reading asks for a card of this type. Additionally, if the Justice card arises in a Libra person's spread, it likely represents that person him or herself.

Tarot Looks at Scorpio...

...and sees the Death card from the Major Arcana. Both are intense, fascinated by transformation, interested in rebirth, enigmatic, changeable, and introspective. They can both also be extremely personal or utterly detached, for they contain so many extremes. If you're a Scorpio conducting a reading for yourself (or if you're reading for someone else who's a Scorpio), choose the Death card to represent yourself (or the Scorpio querent in question) if the reading asks for a card of this type. Additionally, if the Death card arises in a Scorpio person's spread, it likely represents that person him or herself.

Tarot Looks at Sagittarius...

...and sees the Temperance card from the Major Arcana. Both are gifted mediators and social balancers, understanding leaders, and conscious adventurers. If you're a Sagittarius conducting a reading for yourself (or if you're reading for someone who's a Sagittarius), choose the Temperance card to represent yourself (or the Sagittarius querent in question) if the reading asks for a card of this type. Additionally, if the Temperance card arises in a Sagittarius person's spread, it likely represents that person him or herself.

Tarot Looks at Capricorn...

...and sees the Devil card from the Major Arcana. Both are shadowy yet skilled, guarded yet knowledgeable, intense yet internally playful, reflective yet confident, and restrictive yet protective of others. If you're a Capricorn conducting a reading for yourself (or if you're reading for someone who's a Capricorn), choose the Devil card to represent yourself (or the Capricorn querent in question) if the reading asks for a card of this type. Additionally, if the Devil card arises in a Capricorn person's spread, it likely represents that person him or herself.

Tarot Looks at Aquarius...

...and sees the Star card from the Major Arcana. Both are enlightened, optimistic, spiritual, leaders, altruistic, and humanitarian. If you're an Aquarius conducting a reading for yourself (or if you're reading for someone else who's an Aquarius), choose the Star card to represent yourself (or the Aquarius querent in question) if the reading asks for a card of this type. Additionally, if the Star card arises in an Aquarius person's spread, it likely represents that person him or herself.

Tarot Looks at Pisces…

…and sees the Moon card from the Major Arcana. Both are dreamy, idealistic, potentially deluded, intuitive, emotional, strong, compassionate, creative, moody, and subtle. If you're a Pisces conducting a reading for yourself (or if you're reading for some else who's a Pisces), choose the Moon card to represent yourself (or the Pisces querent in question) if the reading asks for a card of this type. Additionally, if the Moon card arises in a Pisces person's spread, it likely represents that person him or herself.

Tarot Looks at Water Signs…

…and sees the suit of Cups. Whether your wateriness comes from your Western zodiac sign (Cancer, Scorpio, and Pisces are water signs), your Eastern zodiac sign (Rat and Pig are water signs), your internal Ayurvedic constitution (a.k.a. – your Dosha (Pitta and Kapha constitutions are water-influenced), or otherwise, those associated with the element of water will connect best with the suit of Cups. If Cups arise for you in a reading, they will signify positivity and alignment on your soul mission or life path. If you're looking for a card to demonstrate yourself as a water sign, choose any of the water sign cards (the Chariot, Death, or the Moon), or choose one of the court/face cards in the suit of Cups.

Tarot Looks at Fire Signs…

…and sees the suit of Wands. Whether your fire energy comes from your Western zodiac sign (Aries, Leo, and Sagittarius are fire signs), your Eastern zodiac sign (Snake and Horse are fire signs), your internal Ayurvedic constitution or Dosha (Pitta is primarily fire-influenced), or otherwise, those associated with the element of fire will connect best with the suit of Wands. If Wands arise for you in a reading, they will signify positivity and alignment on your soul mission or life path. If you're looking for a card to demonstrate yourself as a fire sign, choose any of the fire sign cards (the Emperor, Strength, or Temperance), or choose one of the court cards in the suit of wands.

Tarot Looks at Air Signs...

...and sees the suit of Swords. Whether your airiness comes from your Western zodiac sign (Gemini, Libra, and Aquarius are air signs), your internal Ayurvedic constitution or Dosha (Vata is primarily air-influenced), or otherwise (the Eastern zodiac has no alignment with the element of air; they substitute for elements of metal and wood instead), those associated with the element of air will connect best with the suit of Swords. If Swords arise for you in a reading, they will signify positivity and alignment on your soul mission or life path. If you're looking for a card to demonstrate yourself as an air sign, choose any of the air sign cards (the Lovers, Justice, and the Star), or choose one of the court cards in the suit of Swords.

Tarot Looks at Earth Signs...

...and sees the suit of Pentacles. Whether your earthiness comes from your Western zodiac sign (Taurus, Virgo, and Capricorn are earth signs), your Eastern zodiac sign (Dog, Sheep, Ox, and Dragon are earth signs), your internal Ayurvedic constitution or Dosha (Kapha is primarily earth-influenced), or otherwise, those associated with the element of Earth will connect best with the suit of Pentacles. If Pentacles arise for you in a reading, they will signify positivity and alignment on your soul mission or life path. If you're looking for a card to demonstrate yourself as an earth sign, choose any of the earth sign cards (the Hierophant, the Hermit, or the Devil), or choose one of the court cards in the suit of Pentacles.

Chapter 7: Moving Beyond the Deck

If you're like me, this knowledge about the tarot isn't enough. You're already getting your own deck (or collection of decks), you're working with the knowledge, and you're ready to do something with it! If you're like me, you're interested in thinking about how to turn tarot into a career (or at least a "side hustle").

This chapter is dedicated to helping you follow that path, if you wish to do so. Chapter 7 guides you through what vocational tarot is all about, how to get started, what business options exist, and even a 5-step guide for people that relate to this path. If you're drawn to make your living with the assistance of tarot, this chapter is devoted to you.

Using the Tarot Vocationally

Using a metaphysical practice like tarot to start a financial and lifelong vocation is not the easiest task, but it is a pure, righteous, and high-vibration one. Vocational tarot reading can be a remote job, or it can be extremely up-close and personal, depending on what you're comfortable with. You could run an app, or you could run a shop. You could offer private readings, or you could do public work. You could also spread your gifts through word of mouth and see who comes to you.

When you intend to start a business around metaphysics, or tarot specifically, remember that it's best to diversify. If you have the means, open a metaphysical shop–not just a psychic studio. In that shop, however, offer a section for tarot card readings for whomever desires. If you don't have the means, start small and make as many face-to-face connections with people as possible! You never know who will end up wanting to donate based on your gifts.

How to Get Started

The best way to get started with this goal is to define your basics. Consider the following questions:

- Where and with whom are you willing (and not willing) to work?
- What exactly will you offer? Will there be more than just tarot readings? Will you offer specific spreads only?
- Will you insist on qualifications met by clients beforehand?
- What are you offering that's different from others in your area doing the same thing?
- What will your prices be? How will you collect payment? Will you have any sort of sliding scale for payment? If so, for how long–just until you're established or always?
- How will you promote yourself?
- Will you use social media? If so, which sites?
- Can you program, or do you have a programmer buddy? Can you (or that person) make an app to share your work?
- Can you create a website?
- Have you considered Etsy for your platform to start?
- Is there a social media platform you already have that you can expand to take this venture on?

- How do you imagine your business will grow?
- Are you fearful of taking things online or of doing things in person?

Ask yourself all these questions and more, for it's immeasurably helpful to know where your boundaries are from the start and what your basics of business happen to be.

Business Options

- Offer weekly tarot readings in any public space (to start). Options for spaces to host you include cafes, diners, libraries, parks, and more.
- Pair up with local businesses to host tarot nights for Girls' Nights Out and Date Nights.
- Create an app to share your knowledge.
- Create a podcast or YouTube channel to share your knowledge.
- Make your initial business "storefront" a social media page.
- Start a blog about your knowledge to get your energy out there.
- Similarly, write tarot-inspired or -based articles for local magazines and newspapers.
- You can even try to get your own tarot column in your hometown paper to help promote yourself.
- Buy and establish your own literal storefront that you'll have for just psychic and tarot readings (or for metaphysical materials sales, too).
- Create a website with options for virtual tarot readings via email, for example.
- Design your own tarot deck and try to get it "published."
- Write your own tarot book and work to get that published.
- Create a tarot retreat for high-vibration individuals in your town or city.

- Offer Skype or phone-based sessions and leave fliers with your number around town.
- Find a mentor business owner and pair with him or her to promote your wares.
- Similarly, offer weekly tarot readings at your local bookstore or metaphysical shop.

General 5-Step Guide for Tarot Practitioners in Business

For those of you who are ready to follow this path with tarot and take it seriously, the following guide will hopefully provide the logistical or ideological backbone you need to build this tarot empire for yourself (and others).

Step 1 – Start Small

For those just starting off with this transition, it really helps to start small. Especially if you're not the most confident tarot card reader, working one-on-one with others for a while can really give you the boost of energy, certainty, and privacy that you need to begin trusting yourself deeply with these cards. Keep your expectations of your business low so that you can be easily surprised when things start to take off. You're welcome to start planning the infrastructure of your future business, but I recommend not getting *too* caught up in details at this phase of your journey. The first phase is about exploring the options, meeting some people, doing confident readings, and remembering your passion in the first place.

Step 2 – Start Local

A great way to break into the local scene is to start local and work with business owners whose ethics and vibes align with the energies of tarot. Find a local vegetarian or vegan restaurant and get to know the owner, patrons, and employees! You might find your first clients in this base of people. Furthermore, try metaphysical stores, bookstores of all types, coffee shops, and high-vibration shops of all other kinds. Seek out like-minded people, give them a trial reading, and see if they'll promote your work. Make relationships with local business owners, and you might have a Friday or Saturday space to host readings in no time. Connect with other high-vibration healers in your area, too. If you can find them personally, great! If you have to find them virtually, through social media or otherwise, that's fine too. Make connections with these people for you never know who you'll team up with in the future.

Step 3 – Find a Mentor

You never know who might support you, so don't be afraid to reach out to potential patrons for mentorship, too! Local business owners are wonderful, but you could also start socializing with other lovers of divination in order to find yourself a true metaphysical mentor. In fact, this stage of your journey isn't mandatory, but it can help substantially to develop your future business plan. For example, imagine that you've begun hanging out extensively at the local metaphysical store. You chat up the owner every time you come in, and he or she really appreciates your hard work, your passion, and your budding expertise. With a little more talking, you realize that this person is also devoted to tarot (as well as some other things), and you begin taking weekly lessons with him or her. Voilà-- mentor achieved!

Step 4 – Have Pride

One of the most important steps to perfect before you can start up that future business of yours is that you're going to have to maintain immaculate pride and confidence in yourself, your psychic abilities, and your tarot knowledge. Keep a consistent practice until you truly remember all the card meanings; then, take your skills out into the world and wow some people! When people respond positively, use that good energy to boost your self-image and your sense of pride. If people respond negatively, remind yourself that you probably just accosted them with truth! Don't feel too bad, and don't doubt yourself. No matter how people respond, remember your love of tarot, your careful study of it, and your blossoming passion to share it! You're following your purpose, and that insists you follow your path with pride.

Step 5 – Move on Up

Once you've worked through the first 4 steps, it's time to start increasing your scope. You're making connections with local business owners, and you're establishing a clientele. Now's the time to make a social media page for your work so people can start leaving reviews. If you can afford it, promote your page so that anyone interested in metaphysics nearby will find your business without issue. Promote yourself with fliers, by word of mouth, and through posters placed in public spaces that have sign-ups for readings on them. Grow your business bit by bit, and soon enough, you may find yourself with a space to call your office or even your very own shop! Troubleshoot as you go along by asking customers to provide honest reviews of your work, and as long as you're in touch with your higher self, you'll be sure to succeed.

I applaud anyone who aims to turn his or her love of tarot into a vocation. If you relate to this message, I'm proud of you for finding your passion and for being so willing to work with others as your work in the world. I'm also proud of you for embracing your potential as a healer and teacher of others. I know that things may be bumpy for you in the times ahead, but they'll surely settle out in time.

If you encounter hardship, take a step back, and try to remember why you were so drawn to tarot at first. If you ever feel dejected, remember what you loved about tarot and what it gave you when your work started out. Remember these exciting origins to cure any malaise, disinterest, or imbalance.

Promise me that you'll use your abilities for goodness, healing, and growth, and above all else: promise me you'll never lie to someone during their reading because you think you're protecting him or her. Truth and knowledge are light, and to withhold these things from someone is to shed darkness on that light. You're a light-worker if you feel drawn to tarot as a vocation, and now's the time to put that light to work.

Conclusion

Throughout this book, you've encountered information about the history of tarot, each card in the deck, how to choose and then use your deck, and how tarot can change your life. Now, you've completed reading each chapter, and by making it to the end of the book, you deserve a congratulations! Well done, and thank you for making it to the final pages.

Now, it's time to put all this theory into practice. If you haven't been looking at your deck while you were reading–or if you weren't trying out the spreads, memorization tips, and exercises as you went along–now is the time to start trying everything out!

Get your hands on your own beautiful deck of tarot cards, and let yourself experience their beauty, knowledge, and wisdom first-hand. Sit down with your cards spread out around you and take in their mastery before trying out a few spreads for yourself. It's going to be a beautiful adventure for you, and I wish you nothing but the best.

If you've appreciated this book or found it useful for your tarot practice, please feel free to leave a review on Amazon about what you liked! Similarly, if you think my approach could be strengthened or changed in any way, please let me know about that as well.

Thank you again for making it to the end of *Tarot: An Essential Beginner's Guide to Psychic Tarot Reading, Tarot Card Meanings, Tarot Spreads, Numerology, and Astrology.* I hope you found the experience useful, and I wish you all the best as you journey into tarot for yourself. Good luck!

Check out more books by Kimberly Moon

And another one…